"Whatever colors you have in your mind,
I'll show them to you and you'll see them shine."

– Bob Dylan

eva

Slideaway Sofa Bed

reddot winner 2024

Sit.

Slide.

Snooze.

eva.com.au

Editor
Elizabeth Price
Editor@nevertoosmall.com

Creative Direction
Colin Chee

Art Director
Lara Burke

Editorial Assistant
Eloïse Lachicorée

Proofreading
Penny Craswell

Advertising & Partnerships
James McPherson
james@nevertoosmall.com

Distribution
Ra & Olly
office@raandollyltd.com

Marketing & Operations
Lindsay Barnard
Joel Beath

Front Cover Image
Maria Clara Macrì

Back Cover Image
Paul Kessel

Note card Art
Maria Clara Macrì

Masthead design
Sebby T

ISSN
2982-1002

Publisher
James McPherson
Never Too Small Pty Ltd
292 Wellington Street
Collingwood VIC 3066
Australia

...

We acknowledge the Traditional Owners of the land on which this magazine is published, the Wurundjeri People of the Kulin Nation.

ISSUE 4 CONTRIBUTORS

Words
Andrea & Francesca
Bec Vrana Dickinson
Elizabeth Price
Eloïse Lachicorée
James Shackell
Jana Perković
Kate Kolberg
Kirsten Drysdale
Penny Craswell

...

Artwork & Photography
Alfonso Galán Martínez
Anna Kucera
Carlo Oriente
Denis Esakov
Francesco Stelitano
Gabriele De Cicco
Gonzalo Pardo
JD Chang
Kirthana Selvaraj
Maria Clara Macrì
Michael Wee
Nam Tran
Paul Kessel

...

With special thanks to
ATOMAA
gon architects
La Fotosintesi
Maria Clara Macrì
Paul Kessel
Rachel Lacy
Yin Yin Lee

...

All rights reserved. No part of this publication may be reproduced in whole or in part without permission from the publisher. The views expressed in Never Too Small Quarterly are those of the respective contributors and are not necessarily shared by Never Too Small and its staff.

Printed by C&C Offset Printing. CO. Ltd. in China

Never Too Small
is created by
Colin Chee.

Creative Director
Colin Chee

Managing Director
James McPherson

General Manager
Lindsay Barnard

Head of Digital
Joel Beath

Finance Manager
Petrina Crocker

Video Production
Nam Tran
Jessica Ruasol
Sebastian Tibbs

Social Media & Channel Manager
Alannah Song

For more creative, compact and joyful ways to design and live:

Website
nevertoosmall.com

YouTube
youtube.com/@nevertoosmall

Instagram
@nvtsmall

Books & Publications
nts-store.com

(Right)
Detail from Ricardo Bofill's *Muralla Roja* within the La Manzanera development in Spain's Calpe. Image: Gregori Civera courtesy of Ricardo Bofill Taller de Arquitectura.

What is MUJI?

MUJI was founded in 1980 to realise a vision – to offer products useful to the customer, while retaining balance between life and the objects that make it possible. The concept was born via the intersection of two distinct ideals: no brand (Mujirushi) and the value of good items (Ryohin).

Our focus is to create simple, quality products by thoroughly reviewing manufacturing processes and everyday life. Specifically, we examine each item through three core principles:

1. Selection of materials
2. Streamlining of processes
3. Simplification of packaging

MUJI's emphasis on the intrinsic appeal of an object through rationalisation and meticulous elimination of excess is closely connected to the traditionally Japanese aesthetic of "su" – meaning plain or unadorned – the idea that simplicity is not merely modest or frugal but could possibly be more appealing that luxury. The essence of a MUJI product lies in its flexibility and modesty to fit different lifestyles and individual preferences.

Contents
Issue 4.

016
24 Hours in Madrid with gon architects

Enter the colourful world of gon architects where architecture is used to empower a more joyful mode of living and the bathroom is making a comeback.

030
More than a Rug

Meet the founder of GUR, Célia Esteves and learn how these tactile and colourful beauties are not only helping to preserve Portugal's artisanal weaving heritage, but also celebrating a new generation of artists and designers.

036
Sameness be Damned

We take a moment to pay tribute to Memphis Milano and unpick why its designs remain so fascinating and relevant today.

050
The Home of Photosynthesis

Giuseppe Ponzo and Julie Nebout are the humans behind Naples architecture studio La Fotosintesi. We visit them in their home and find we never want to leave.

062
Small Home: Poerio

We had to leave their home, but we got to see another one: La Fotosintesi's redesign of a small home and medical practice in Naples fearlessly embraces its client's passion for "interiors with significant character" and the colour brown.

074
Small Home: Pine

Nicholas Gurney's trademark approach to spatial organisation and custom furniture solutions have transformed this Sydney apartment into a home that responds more intuitively to the lives of its creative residents.

086
Wild, Wild Colour

One of Pine's creative residents is artist Kirthana Selvaraj who, once upon a time, only worked in charcoal. Colour seemed like a foreboding and untamable beast to Kirthana but one day, everything changed.

094
Small Home: Casa Desa

In Jun Ong's Kuala Lumpur apartment the contentment of his feline companions carried as much weight in driving design decisions as Jun's desire to craft an open and welcoming home ideal for a passionate home cook, entertainer and collector.

107
Sunkissed Sheets

A short story on the superiority of sundried sheets.

108
A Shared Stillness

We discuss the shared aesthetics and mutual admiration between Japanese and Scandinavian design with Jonas Bjerre-Poulsen, co-founder of Danish multidisciplinary practice Norm Architects.

114
A Soft Side

Ever wondered what plates and bowls inspired by the medieval myth of Cockaigne look like? The answer is seductive and smooth. Meet Layla Cluer of Softedge Studio and her very pleasing porcelain.

120
A Matter of Context

Ben Mooney understands the power of context. His gift for styling and his store in Melbourne are an enchanting window into how to mix vintage and antiques with contemporary design and how to make our homes more interesting.

132
What we do with the Shadows

He may have been accused of "only designing homes for rich people" ("and horses.") but the grandfather of Mexican modernism, Luis Barragán, changed Latin architecture forever.

198
No Glass. No Pineapples.

Glass. It's so ubiquitous we sometimes forget it's there. Well, no more. It's time to give glass the credit and respect it deserves (especially if you like pineapples).

210
The Language of Colour

An interview with the founders of Dutch multidisciplinary studio Raw Color, who are driven by a singular determination to spread more vibrancy across the world of design.

220
The Village in the Sky

The story of Barcelona's ambitious labyrinth-like 1970s social housing project: Walden 7.

234
A Directory of Colour

Our curation of brands, retailers, designers and makers who are a dependable source of colour.

144
Look at all the Lonely People

Mannequins as housemates is certainly one way to go, but what else can we do about urban loneliness? And why are we so lonely to begin with?

153
Meet Paul Kessel

The vibrant New York City street scenes captured by Paul Kessel work on you like a brilliant piece of music – the more time you spend with them, the more the layers reveal themselves and suddenly, you're entranced.

162
Colour Cheat Sheet

Warning: colour expert Rachel Lacy, doesn't like white walls. Not one bit. Rachel shares her expertise on working with colour in small spaces and her feelings about white plates.

174
When Design met Colour

When these two got together things got a little wild. It also freed the rest of us from a life lived "housed in dreary, grey-beige conformity, mortally afraid of using colours."

178
The Everyday Architect

While it's invisible to many, architect Chatchavan Suwansawat believes Thai urban vernacular design – street-level creativity, ingenuity and resourcefulness in Bangkok – could be the key to many of the city's challenges.

188
Inspiration and Ideas for Colour and Cleverness

Some clever people with clever ideas who have inspired us and we think might inspire you too.

190
Inhabiting a House of Crimson Flames

Reflections from the residents of a Milanese apartment (designed by our good friends at ATOMAA) that finds its climax in a magical flame-red column.

196
Too Good for its Own Good

What happens to design when it becomes *too* good?

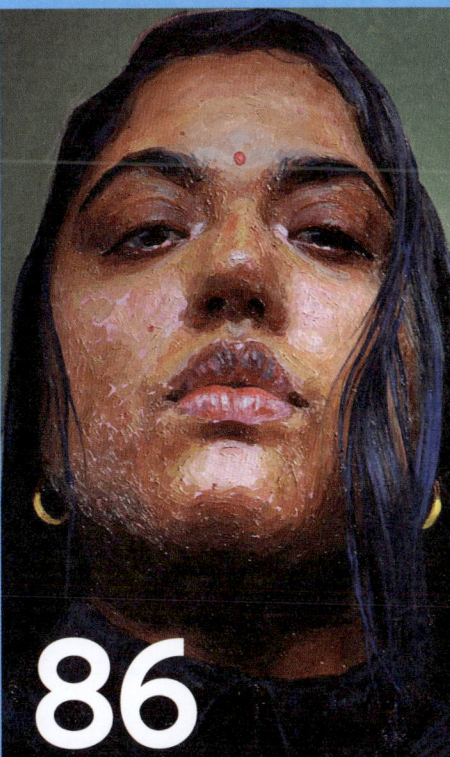

EDITOR'S LETTER

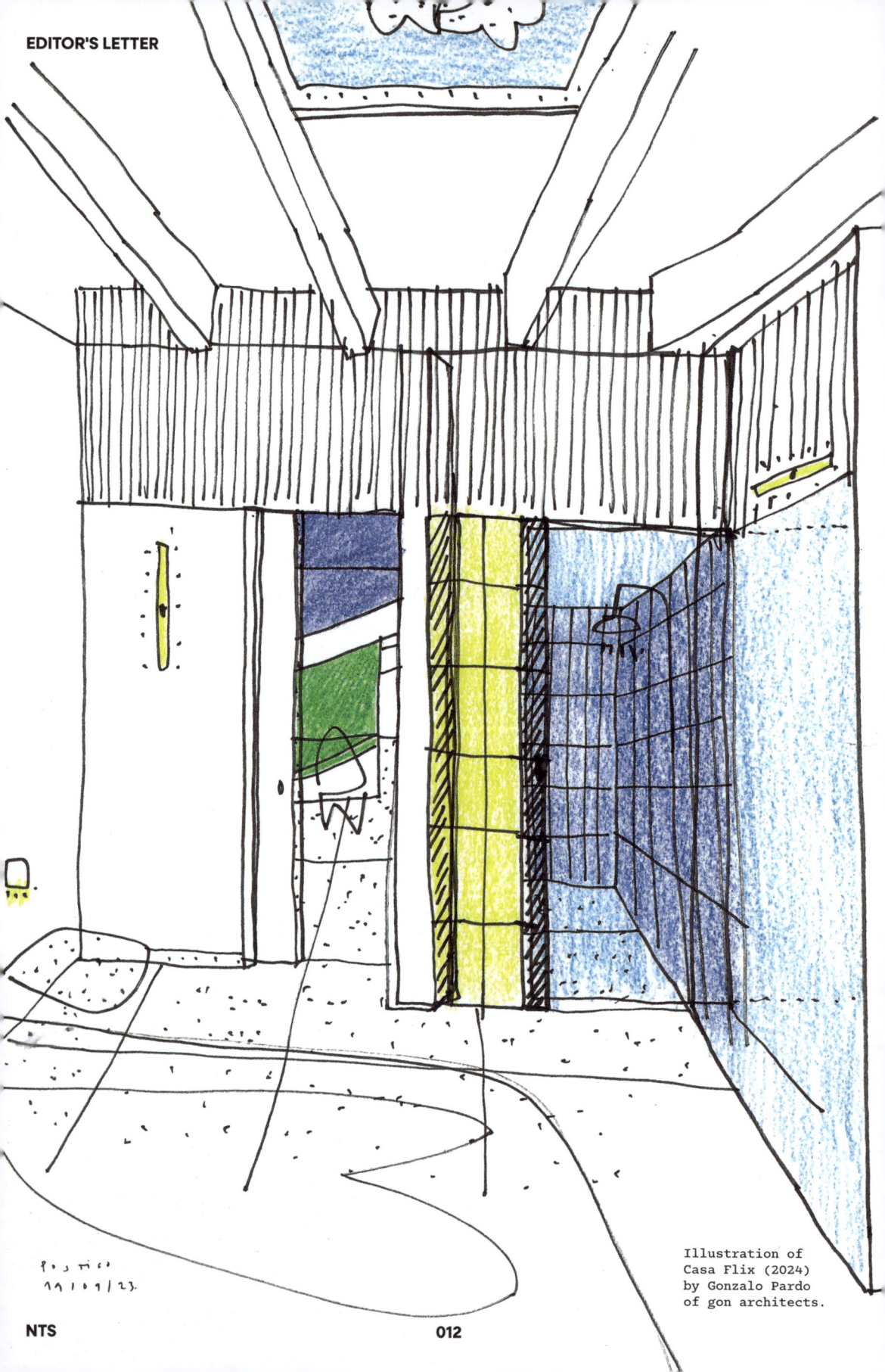

Illustration of Casa Flix (2024) by Gonzalo Pardo of gon architects.

EDITOR'S LETTER

For all the bad wrap social media gets, for a small team tucked away on a big island down under, it's often our portal of discovery. Our cover stars, Julie and Giuseppe of La Fotosintesi, for instance, stopped us in our Instagram tracks many months ago with the image you will find inside the front cover of this magazine. The image is from a photoshoot capturing Julie and Giuseppe's design with their *L'Appuntamento* project. It was a collaboration with artists local to the pair in Naples, Italy with a view to creating a hybrid shoot merging architecture, fashion, and design. This subversive merging of worlds certainly captured our attention. Along with all the colour. As we explored La Fotosintesi's work further we discovered a command of colour that felt entirely new to us.

We have a little rule at Never Too Small that the story gets the run it deserves. That is to say, why contain a story to a single feature and a mere 10-12 pages if it has the merit to sing and thrill across many more? This is why, after meeting Julie and Giuseppe on our cover and seeing a glimpse of their genius inside our font cover, you will meet them again in their home *Paradisiello* in Naples **(p50)** in a dreamlike photoshoot shot and directed by our new best friend, Italian photographer Maria Clara Macrì (words by James Shackell). And you will meet them directly after, too, in one of our Small Home features – amongst all those rich blues, reds and browns – in Poerio **(p62)**.

Julie and Giuseppe are not our only repeat appearances either. There's Paul Kessel – a street photographer whose layered city scenes make up our photographic feature on **p153** but not before his pandemic-time self-portraits bring humour and pathos to James Shackell's feature on the state of urban loneliness **(p144)**. And it doesn't end there either. During the research for one of our other Small Home features, this time centred on Nicholas Gurney's *Pine*, we became entranced by a painting that appears in the marvellous photos shot by Michael Wee. Nic informed me that Kirthana Selveraj, one of the home's residents, was a Sydney-based painter. "You should interview her," he said. And indeed we felt we must. You'll see Kirthana in her home on **p74** and again in her studio with her vibrant paintings on **p86**.

In addition to these common threads, you may well notice another – colour. Colour was the basis of our infatuation with La Fotosintesi and it's a force that animates and plays the role of muse in many of the stories that follow. It's a key character in the homes designed by our dear friends at gon architects **(p16)** just as it was for the grandfather of Mexican modernism, Luis Barragán. It's woven into the mischievous rugs made by Célia Esteves **(p30)**, it was in the DNA of Memphis Milano **(p36)** and its key to Chatchavan Suwansawat's campaign as he champions everyday design, in all its vibrancy, in Bangkok **(p178)**. It's 'taken seriously' in A House of Crimson Flames **(p190)** and by the multidisciplinary Dutch studio, Raw Color **(p210)** too. We learn that it wasn't always this way though. With *When Design Met Colour* (it sounds like a love story, and I suppose in some ways, it is), Penny Craswell explores what this marriage meant for the world of design and for the rest of us too **(p174)**.

Danish designer Verner Panton once professed "The main purpose of my work is to provoke people into using their imagination ... Most people spend their lives housed in dreary, grey-beige conformity, mortally afraid of using colours." This idea of being *fearful* of colour does surface more than once within the stories that follow, but these appearances are vastly outnumbered by those that refer to the sense of joy, meaning or vitality that colour conjures in our lives. So, if you're like me, with a white wall or two, don't be afraid. Turn to page **p162** where we've engaged the expertise of paint colour consultant and straight-talker Rachel Lacy to build out a *Colour Cheat Sheet* for small spaces and build all of our bravery with colour.

We hope you enjoy it all and as always, if the mood strikes, let us know what you think.

Elizabeth Price
editor@nevertoosmall.com

bonny

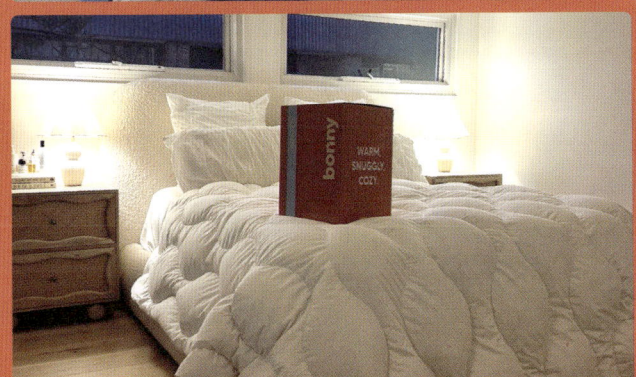

Making doonas cool, so you can sleep warm.

Airless Feel. Audacious Quality.
Thanks to our best in class down filling, our doonas are fluffier, lighter and cosier.

All our down is verified at 800+ fill power, plus, with 90% down and only 10% feather fibres, you won't find any prickly quills - just long lasting, cloud like fluffiness.

Cosy, Cloud-Like, and Cuddly.
In our mission to develop the best doona on the market, we've spent countless nights trialling dozens of samples in all different climates and situations: on our own, with our partners, even with our pets!

In this we have created the most functional, feel good doona you could ever dream of (or in).

Meticulously Test. Impossibly Clean.
Perfectionists, meticulous, neurotic — call us what you want. We clean our down until its completely hypoallergenic.

Our results are verified with Turbidity and Oxygen tests on every batch using bluesign® approved detergents (just sayin').

Ethically sourced, responsibly made.
Simply put: the cosiest, fluffiest doonas on the market come with peace of mind, too.

Thanks to our RDS certification, we ensure that Bonny's down never involves live plucking or force-feeding. Instead, our down is responsibly sourced as a byproduct of the poultry industry and would have otherwise gone to waste.

BONNY.COM.AU

24 HOURS in MADRID with GON ARCHITECTS

WORDS JANA PERKOVIĆ
PORTRAITS ALFONSO GALÁN MARTÍNEZ

How you cook, bathe and even how you have sex. These are crucial clues when designing your perfect home, as Jana Perković finds when she enters the colourful world of gon architects.

"When I started my doctoral research in 2016," Gonzalo Pardo, the founder of gon architects, tells me, "I wanted to know how we, in developed countries, had arrived at an open-plan kitchen."

Gonzalo was already working on small residential projects. "In a small home, you have to erase, erase, erase, make fast decisions. You have to articulate a house in a very small space. What you take out is more important than what you put in." He was looking at *MasterChef* and wondering how cooking had become so important. "For example, in Ancient Rome there was no kitchen – just a public surface in the street called tabernae, from which people sold food. In Renaissance villas, the kitchen was in the basement. Then it starts migrating to the centre of the house."

Gonzalo became obsessed with charting how cultures have changed with time, pulling the home along. His award-winning PhD thesis starts in the Paleolithic with the discovery of the fire, and ends with the air-fryer. "Today, the kitchen is often a large, central room, but it's increasingly disconnected from cooking. It has become a room for socialising, enjoying life." As a non-cook, he finds this fascinating: he could easily live in a kitchenless house.

"The bathroom, on the other hand, goes the opposite way: to the periphery." He shows me image after image of large, communal baths that were ubiquitous in medieval cities. Strangers bathed, ate and enjoyed music together. "It all ended with the Black Death. Suddenly, the authorities said that air and water spread diseases – particularly water, because it opened pores. For the next 200 years, everyone covered up their whole body." Bathrooms disappeared – there isn't, for example, a single one in Versailles – reduced to a small portable chamber pot. It is only now, he thinks, that the bathroom is becoming a social space again, as we sit on our toilets scrolling on social media.

It is worth understanding, he says, that architects were always the least important people at the table – the home was shaped by engineers, by politics, by social trends, such as the emancipation of women. "When we understand this cultural history, we can be more open-minded in our designs."

> Gonzalo's designs are nothing if not open-minded – and the bathroom, I sense, is his true passion. Water is often the protagonist of his designs:

the central glass shower that illuminates Casa Flix (2024) like a lantern; the small pool under a large skylight that adjoins the living room in his own G House (2018); the exquisite open bathroom that spills into the corridor of Sequencehouse (2020) and becomes a walkable, sociable space. Such expansive spaces for enjoyment and self-care are unusual in small homes, which often have to be sternly functional – and it is this playful, hedonistic spirit that attracts clients to him. For his new project, a client asked for a bathroom filled with greenery. She wants, he said, "to bathe in a jungle", like in Henri Rousseau's 1910 oil painting 'The Dream'.

· · ·

(Right)
Gonzalo Pardo, the founder of gon architects is passionate about enabling different and joyful ways of living through architecture.

(Below)
Gonzalo's PhD thesis explored how bathrooms were communal affairs where strangers bathed, ate and enjoyed music together in medieval cities as opposed to the compact, private and utilitarian spaces they've become. Image: courtesy of gon architects.

(Top left)
Inside the gon architecture studio in Madrid.

(Top right)
Playful details complement the warm and relaxed atmosphere in the studio where "banter and laughter fill the air".

(Bottom right)
From left: Gonzalo, María Camila Martínez (Maclas), Carol Linares and María Cecilia Cordero (Coti).

(Above)
From left: Carol Linares, María Camila Martínez (Maclas), María Cecilia Cordero (Coti) and Gonzalo.

Compared to other European capitals, or even Barcelona, Madrid is a uniquely forgettable city. It looks a bit like Paris, but with all the landmarks taken out: wide boulevards, tall buildings, no orientation points. It is the second-biggest city in the EU, its fourth largest urban economy – but if we played charades, or Pictionary, what would you draw if you had to draw me Madrid?

Some of it is due to history. In 1561, King Philip II got tired of touring his disjointed Spanish possessions on horseback – itinerant courts were by then seen as an outdated, medieval practice. Philip fancied himself a modern leader, with an interest in modern urbanism, which in late Renaissance meant public plazas, a grid of wide streets, geometry, symmetry. So he chose a provincial town, smack-bang in the geographical centre of Spain, and built there an administrative centre of his empire. Madrid, in other words, was the Canberra[1] of its time.

I feel this acutely while I'm circling a nondescript building in a nondescript neighbourhood, looking for gon architects' office. There seems to be no care given to the public spaces, nor to the image they project. Gon is a busy office, currently working across Spain, and increasingly Europe, on some 20 projects, ranging from cabinet handles to apartment buildings. I am expecting a flashy office in a hip neighbourhood. Instead, I am in a residential street with a primary school at one end. The only commercial signage is for a ground-floor photocopy shop. Maria Camila Martinez (also known as Maclas), gon's communications coordinator, has to come down to find me.

"It's true, we don't have big monuments," Gonzalo tells me. "Madrid isn't special in that way. But it's very special in other ways. You will see."

"Madrid is a mess," agrees Carol Pierina Linares, who has been something of Gonzalo's right hand for the past 6-7 years. "In Barcelona, the city hires people who make sure that the level of public architecture is very fine. In Madrid, we're missing public policies that really care about architecture."

The contrast between the bland city outside, and the inventive, forward-thinking realm I have just entered, couldn't be starker. Gon's team has largely come through the interdisciplinary, open-minded Master of Architectural Communication at Madrid's polytechnic (MACA), where Gonzalo, then Carol, have taught. Their thinking is broad, with references ranging from Georges Perec's wordplay novels and the mid-century projects of Ray and Charles Eames, to sociological studies. ("I think all of us could be in another profession if we wanted to," Carol muses.) And there is a whimsy and playfulness that infuses their universe. Casa Flix was inspired by Wes Anderson movies. They have made an apartment entirely decked out in a particular shade of mint green used by Prada (Menta, 2021). They have turned a shopfront into a pull-out Latin American street food cart in a bright lime colour (Limeñita, 2022). And in their office, a large model of their latest apartment building is being attacked by a dinosaur figurine.

It's a young and international office: apart from Carol and María (Maclas), there is María (Coti) and Maria (the Greek), all sitting around one big desk. Carol and Coti are Venezuelan, Maclas from Colombia. The atmosphere is warm and relaxed. The company Slack is a constant stream of memes. Banter and laughter fill the air, punctured by a loud hourly chirp.

"This is our bird clock!" says Gonzalo. "It's a different bird sound every hour, and you have to guess the bird." It's their office game, he adds. Carol pipes in: "There is one bird that sounds like a pig!"

. . .

Gonzalo graduated in 2008, straight into the global financial crisis, which hit Spain particularly hard. The construction sector collapsed, leaving some 4 million vacant homes and a youth unemployment rate of 55 per cent. "The generation before us graduated and expected to immediately build buildings," he says. "We all had to look for other types of work." He was among the lucky ones, winning a major public competition straight out of university. Still, he was part of a generation that branched out into research, teaching and curation – and in the process, developed a more politically and environmentally aware approach to architecture.

---

[1] Australia's capital city, like Madrid, was purpose built as an administrative centre and let's just say evidence indicates this is not the kind of beginning that ends in an immediately charming and characterful city. In Bill Bryson's book *Down Under* (2000) he proposed the following peppy slogan for the city: "Canberra: Why Wait for Death?".

We are eating lunch at Run Run Run, a restaurant with its own greenhouse, showers and lockers for the local running club, a building-manifesto to local food production, community and sustainability. It was designed by Andres Jaque, another prominent representative of the 'crisis generation'. Looking outside from its mayhem of colours, textures, plants and customers, the drab street is another universe. The generational gap is palpable.

Maclas is organising me a ticket for an awards gala that evening. gon has been nominated for Casavera (2024), a shopfront in Valencia refurbished into an accessible family home for Elies, wheelchair-bound entrepreneur and activist, his artist wife Aurora, and their daughter Vera.

"In housing competitions, Madrid still talks about apartments 'for a married couple'," Carol tells me, visibly miffed. "Come on! Not only married people need housing!" They have completed accessible homes, homes for a single mum, for a single woman, for co-living, she says. "There are different ways of living. We try to enable them through architecture – that's where we find the richness of life."

(Bottom)
One of Gonzalo's illustrations for gon architects' award-winning project, Casavera.

Gonzalo tells me they start every project by interviewing the client in depth about how they live: how they cook, how they have sex, whether they prefer a bath or a shower...

"Sorry, wait," I interrupt. "You ask them how they have sex?"

"Well, yes," Gonzalo nods. "It's really important!

And they go: 'Oh, uh, do we have to answer?' Yes, you have to answer." There is something genuine and charming in Gonzalo's explanation, and by now we're all roaring with laughter. "But," he continues, "it's really interesting what we discover. Many of them have been living their lives as their father and mother have told them. They discover, for example, that, if they cook a lot, they can have a big kitchen in the middle of the house. 'Can I really have this?' Of course you can!

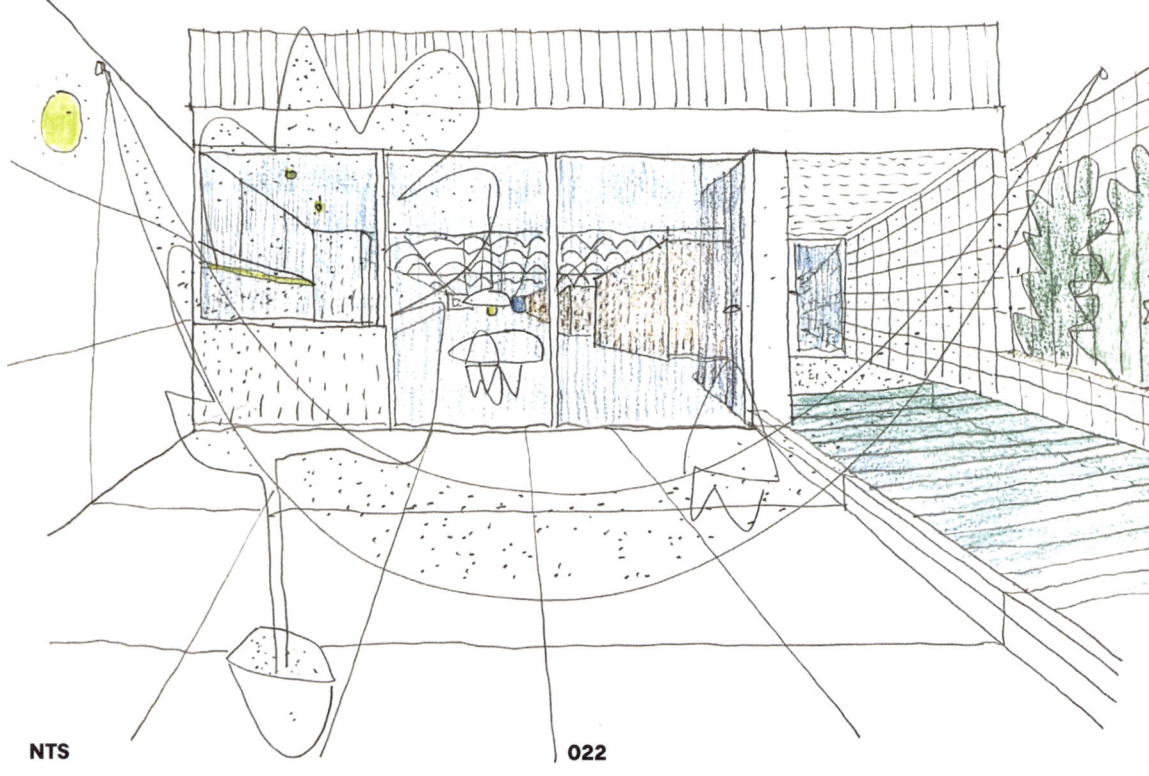

Casavera embraces "the logic of local materials and proximity" evoking both the nearby Mediterranean and the character of its local neighbourhood of El Cabanyal with a dominant materials palette of clay, wood, and ceramics. Image: Imagen Subliminal.

"For example, 'I'd love to have a bath in the jungle' – that's the beginning of the story of this person's home.."

Carol nods: "Everything starts with the story of the client, and ends with the story of their house."

"And every aesthetic choice is the consequence of the narrative," Maclas pipes in.

"In the end," says Gonzalo, "the name 'gon' could stand for 'great office of narratives'. A good work of architecture is like a good book."

Take Casavera. "It's a story about the Mediterranean," he says, about the salt-resistant materials of the area and the historical trading neighbourhoods of Valencia, as well as about Elies and Aurora. "If I made a house for myself there, it would be very different. But it's a house for them – I think, one of our best projects."

Casavera started off as a long and narrow ground-floor space with a small back patio. The new design has wide passageways, an accessible bathroom, and a long skinny swimming pool for Elies. Though accessibility was key to its design, the house comes across as an easy, modern coastal home for a family with a small child.

"And the four cats!" Maclas adds.

"They were the bosses," Carol shakes her head.

Gonzalo nods. "Every meeting was like: 'So, what have you thought for Lupito?' 'Lupito?' 'My cat. How is he going to go from the kitchen to the bathroom?'"

"In the end, we designed two circulation plans: one for the humans and one for the cats," Carol remembers. "With their own small doors, climbing structures and ways to get across furniture."

Later that night, Maclas and I traverse a confusing metro station and a totally nondescript plaza to get to our gala. We watch Gonzalo collect the award – no surprises there, Casavera is brilliant – and I wonder how many people know that the actual client was Lupito.

. . .

The next morning, Gonzalo, Maria (the Greek) and I dash through Madrid's historical centre on a tour of half a dozen gon homes. Some of the owners are there to greet us, others have left the key to Gonzalo – or in a nearby bar, allowing us to also grab cheap, delicious treats. On this morning, Madrid seems like a friendly village. Everyone we meet is smiling, joking – lovely. I remember what Maclas said to me: "All of Gonzalo's clients become his friends." Gonzalo brings a little present to Cecilia, who lets us into her brilliant attic apartment, Casa Gialla (2023). The entire building was renovated 30 years ago in chalet style – dark wood, exposed beams – but Cecilia's apartment is awash in light, with a warm yellow wall that hides clutter away in built-in cupboards.

> "In medieval times, there were no separate rooms, just one room with a big cupboard," Gonzalo tells us. "Depending on the time of day, residents would bring out stuff for cooking, for sleeping… It was like a magic box, used to organise the space."

Cecilia gushes about her outdoor bath and shower. "From March until November, I only have showers outside! But even in winter, with a bit of chill, the hot water is amazing." She got her inspiration from Gonzalo's own apartment. "It has the same feeling, of taking the time to enjoy the place where you live."

(Top)
The central courtyard in Casavera is the heart of the home and can be enjoyed all year round on account of Valencia's mild climate. Its pool acts as a thermodynamic device, helping to regulate the home's temperature while also reflecting light into its living spaces. Image: Imagen Subliminal.

(Bottom)
Casavera has been designed as a home "at the service of those who live in it". Image: Imagen Subliminal.

(Top and bottom)
Sequencehouse is designed to express a succession of domestic narratives linked to the basic actions of cooking, sleeping, resting, working and self care. These zones are each defined by transitions in colour and lighting.
Image: Imagen Subliminal.

(Middle)
"The exquisite open bathroom that spills into the corridor of Sequencehouse" (2020) to become a walkable, sociable space.
Image: Imagen Subliminal.

I start to see a pattern. The challenge in Madrid is not size; some apartments are fairly spacious. But all began as poorly designed, leftover spaces that made everyday life uncomfortable. Some were all corridor, others very dark. The last one, Maison Latomet (2025), started off as a narrow, poorly built duplex. "The feng shui was terrible," says Philippe, the owner. "And it was built with no insulation at all. I had been freezing here for five years."

Gonzalo agrees. "It was not an easy flat."

It is an easy flat now – it has the vibe of a large, relaxed country house, of the kind where you can invite a bunch of friends, and they will all find places to lounge without getting in each other's way. Philippe had wanted to turn his pocket home into a place to host friends and family; miraculously, gon architects has made that possible. The staircase doubles up as a shelf and seating, one wall fully opens to the large terrace, and the diagonal view of the garden extends to the open space upstairs. In the shower, a tiny window offers an exhilarating view over the rooftops. It's details like these that give Gonzalo's apartments such a sense of delight. "We always try to convince clients to do the things we know they'll like," he shrugs, modestly.

A wall of yellow cabinetry and shelving separates the bedroom from the multifunctional kitchen meals and living space in Casa Gialla (2022). Taking cues from medieval dwellings where "...there were no separate rooms, just one room with a big cupboard ... like a magic box, used to organise the space." Image: Imagen Subliminal.

The outdoor shower and bath on the terrace of Casa Gialla converts to a generous space to lounge with a mattress that covers the bath. The home was designed to favour "the unexpected and contemplative life." Image: Imagen Subliminal.

G house (2018) Gonzalo's own home, which he calls "the most livable house", breaks all the rules for how a house should be in order to be a home geared for happiness. Image: Imagen Subliminal.

(Right)
Water is often the protagonist of Gonzalo's designs such as the central glass shower that illuminates Casa Flix (2024) like a lantern. Image: Imagen Subliminal.

"The narrative of this house is exterior," says Gonzalo later, while we're drinking French wine and enjoying Madrid's warm winter sun. "This house wants to be an exterior house."

"It's a very convivial house," Philippe nods. "Everyone finds their own favourite place to sit. But space is also about the nice moments you have together with dear people. It was important to me that you could forget the house, and just enjoy life."

Our last stop is Gonzalo's own home, G House, which adjoins Philippe's. "Two years ago, I was going to sleep when I heard a loud party. I went out really angry, and knocked on his door: 'The music!'" Gonzalo mimics a disgruntled late-night frown. The next day, he found a bottle of Champagne at his door. "I went over and said, 'No no, let's drink it together.'" They began having dinners.

"One night, after a few glasses of wine, I said: 'Philippe, I have to tell you one truth: your home is terrible.' He said: 'What?! Why would you say that?' 'Because it's terrible.' 'What should I do?' 'Renovate it.' 'Who can do it?' I said: 'Me.'"

Is this how you get your clients?, I ask. Gonzalo nods. "Clients appreciate clarity."

Minutes later, we climb the blue staircase to Gonzalo's home. He calls it 'the most livable house' and it's hard not to agree. It is a fully open-plan attic apartment with big windows, two terraces, a green wall, and a bath in the living room. There is a hammock in front of the TV. Gonzalo brings a huge bean bag for me to curl into, in front of the fireplace.

G House breaks all the rules for how a house should be, yet every person I spoke to was inspired by it, its irreverence and playfulness, to be braver in designing a home that really makes them happy: in how they cook, how they bathe, and yes, how they have sex. What a great way to be an architect, I think to myself.

In the end, Gonzalo's designs achieve something rare and remarkable: they take difficult spaces, and make them seem both larger and more full of life.

I remember the 1944 drawing by Charles Eames, 'What is a House?', that portrayed the home as a sum of everyday functions: film-viewing, kite-flying, card-playing, listening to records, shaking cocktails, lounging on comfy furniture. It's that same playful spirit that animates these delightful homes.

Soon I will have to return home. Maria will lead me back to Plaza de España, where I passed the day before, and I will have literally no recollection of having ever been there. The souvenir shop at Madrid airport will sell Star Wars merch and Pringles. Yet Gonzalo is right, I have seen what makes Madrid special – uncovered its secret charms. It's not the monuments that make a city. It's the people who invite you into their homes, offering conviviality, laughter and friendship. It seems this city is not so forgettable after all.

MORE THAN A RUG

We first came across GUR and its founder, Célia Esteves, more than two years ago when we were styling our newly-renovated studio and fell in love with the dramatic 'Fringe Rug' by Pascal Hien (not the name it's known by in our studio, but I'll leave you to fill in those blanks). These joyful little rugs pack quite the punch. Beyond injecting colour, playfulness and instant tactility into your space, they're made from textile waste, they help to preserve Portugal's artisanal weaving heritage, and provide a global platform for a new generation of artists and designers.

INTERVIEW ELIZABETH PRICE
IMAGES COURTESY OF GUR

Hi Célia, where did you grow up?

My hometown is Viana do Castelo (in northern Portugal). Viana is a small city, very friendly and surrounded by nature: mountains, river and sea.

It's known for its rich – and well preserved – Portuguese traditional handicraft culture, such as traditional gold jewellery, embroidery, weaving and lace. We're very proud of our heritage and we celebrate our culture every year with a folklore festival where people show their best traditional costumes and handwork.

What was it like growing up there?

I grew up outside, playing with mud, sticks and picking wild berries; a privilege that is difficult to offer to our kids today. I also had the privilege of closely experiencing crafts and handwork which greatly influenced my professional career. I have memories from my early years of hand-woven rugs like these laid on the floor. They were quite common in the everyday life of Portuguese people.

What is GUR? How did it come to be?

It was an exhibition in my hometown that I was invited to join in 2012 that brought me to my weaver Claudia Vilas Boas, and handmade rugs. The exhibition aimed to build a bridge between young designers and artisans from the region, using traditional handicrafts and techniques to create new works together. The result of this first experience brought me great joy, so I decided to invite more creative friends to join, and entitled the project GUR. Just like the project, the word GUR reflects the transformation and reuse of the word RUG.

1.

2.

3.

4.

Célia Esteves (centre) with her weaver and longtime collaborator Claudia (left) and weaver Anabela (right) at work in their workshop in Viana do Castelo.

1. *Watching You* by Sebastian Anastasiei. 2. *Hairy Legs* by Guglielmo Brambilla. 3. *Jesus Cisneros I*. 4. GUR x FAM. 5. *Mantraste I*. 6. *Fringe Rug* by Pascal Hien. 7. *Your Father* by Bráulio Amado. 8. *Bernardo P. Carvalho II*, GUR x Planeta Tangerina.

Célia Esteves.

What did you set out to achieve with GUR?

GUR transforms a traditional weaving technique into products that represent not only contemporary style and aesthetics but the essence of traditional handicraft with young minds. I invite different creatives such as illustrators, designers and artists from all over the world to collaborate, which makes GUR like a platform for creation and for people whose work I admire.

How are your rugs made?

Portuguese rugs are made of pieces of cotton plus randomly mixed with other textile waste. The combination of all kinds of colours thus makes them unique. Colourful stripes or plain bright colours with traditional patterns created by an embossing technique are also very common. In many countries, rugs made of rags actually embodied a kind of folk wisdom years ago in the era of material scarcity.

GUR also follows Portuguese rugs traditions, using cotton wastes from the textile industry and traditional wooden handlooms in a sustainable way in order not to burden the earth. We carefully select 100 percent cotton from textile waste as our material in order to ensure higher quality and durability. It takes around four to 15 hours to produce a GUR rug depending on the design and technique.

Tell us about the weavers you work with… how long have they been doing what they do?

I have been working with weaver Claudia Vilas Boas since the beginning and it is her knowledge that allows me to explore the technique and its potential. Claudia has been weaving since a young age, she chose weaving as a career at the age of 15. After 12 years, I still feel like her apprentice. I work with five weavers from different workshops with various weaving techniques. In recent years, GUR has kept expanding its range of materials, introducing linen and cotton rag to make small and big tapestries.

How do you find and choose the designers/artists/illustrators you work with?

I'm lucky to be surrounded by good and talented friends who are working on art and illustrations. Two of them had an illustration gallery called Dama Aflita which was the first one in this field with monthly exhibitions in Porto where you could see and meet international artists. I started to invite my friends to collaborate on GUR and asked them to help by inviting artists that I liked and whose works are possible to weave. At some point, I started being contacted by those who wanted to collaborate with me. I've done more than 200 collaborations now. I like the idea that GUR has become global.

rugbygur.com

SAMENESS BE DAMNED

WORDS JAMES SHACKELL
IMAGES COURTESY OF MEMPHIS MILANO

IN 1980, A SMALL DESIGN COLLECTIVE FROM MILAN SPARKED THE POSTMODERNIST MOVEMENT AND CHALLENGED THE VERY IDEA OF 'GOOD TASTE'. SEVEN YEARS LATER, THEY DISBANDED. WELCOME TO THE WEIRD AND WONDERFUL WORLD OF MEMPHIS MILANO.

*Now the bricks lay on Grand Street
Where the neon madmen climb.
They all fall there so perfectly
It all seems so well timed.
An' here I sit so patiently
Waiting to find out what price
You have to pay to get out of
Going through all these things twice.*

Bob Dylan

Even in a chock-a-block 20th century calendar, the year 1980 seems particularly busy and significant. It marked the fall of disco and the early stirrings of New Wave, the assassination of John Lennon and the launch of the Rubix Cube. In 1980, Saddam Hussein invaded Iran, Reagan beat the political snot out of Jimmy Carter, and the world got its first 24-hour news channel, CNN. That year, the World Health Organisation announced arguably the single greatest humanitarian achievement of the century – the eradication of smallpox.

And on December 11, 1980, in the living room of his home in Milan, painter, designer and moustachioed ex-soldier Ettore Sottsass gathered a bunch of colleagues to discuss (what he saw as) the problem with 'modern' design.

In the room were some of the most talented creatives in Europe: radical French architect Martine Bedin, visionary Italian designer Aldo Cibic, award-winning industrial designer Michele De Lucchi – who these days spends his seventies carving wooden houses, armed with nothing but a chainsaw – plus Nathalie Du Pasquier, Matteo Thun and George J. Sowden. It was one of those rooms, and those moments, in which you would have paid good *liras* to be a fly on the wall.

While the designers tossed ideas around, and the sun sank behind the Alps, Bob Dylan's 1966 track *Stuck Inside of Mobile with the Memphis Blues Again* played over and over in the background.

This little gathering marked the spiritual beginning of one of the most controversial artistic collectives of the last 50 years: Memphis Milano, also known as the Memphis Group.

There's always been some debate over the origins of the name. Some say 'Memphis' was lifted from the Dylan track, stuck on a loop during that first meeting. Others say it was chosen because it's the city where Elvis Presley lived (not to be confused with the capital of Ancient Egypt). Whatever the case, pretty soon some other big names had joined the fray, including Andrea Branzi, Shiro Kuramata, Marco Zanini, Peter Shire, Gerard Taylor, Masanori Umeda, Arquitectonica, Michael Graves, Hans Hollein, Arata Isozaki and Javier Mariscal.

About nine months later, on 19 September 1981, at the gallery Arc '74, during Milan's *Salone del Mobile*, Memphis came out to the world. It was their first exhibition: 55 pieces of furniture and industrial design that smashed everyone's pre-conceived notions of good design, or even good taste. A few months after that, over 400 journals were practically buzzing with Memphis articles, dissections, critiques and martini-fuelled diatribes.

Modernism was officially dead in the water. Postmodernism, whatever that was, had arrived.

*Oh, the ragman draws circles
Up and down the block.
I'd ask him what the matter was
But I know that he don't talk.
And the ladies treat me kindly
And furnish me with tape.
But deep inside my heart
I know I can't escape.*

Bob Dylan

Throw a blanket over some of the most recognisable style cues of the 1980s – loud, obnoxious colour blocking, Pop Art, the liberal use of hot pink and electric blue, a weird fascination with techno-futurism, abstract geometric forms, maximalism in all things, especially perms – and you can trace them all back to Memphis Milano. Well, except the hair thing. The collective was a very deliberate attack on the form-follows-function austerity of mid-century modernism, where a thing's inherent *goodness* correlated directly to stuff like ease-of-use, convenience and straight-lined simplicity. Yawn.

"When I was young, all we ever heard about was functionalism, functionalism, functionalism,"

The members of Memphis Milano pictured in the Tawaraya Ring, designed by member Masanori Umeda in 1981. Umeda's aim was to create a domestic "boxing ring" that was "a space that is furniture at the same time," and a ring "for intellectual combat." The ring is based on the proportions of the traditional Japanese woven tatami mat.

Ettore Sottsass with one of the collective's most iconic designs: *Carlton* (1981). *Carlton* embodies Memphis's break from rationalism and its playful and colourful spirit. The piece functions as both a bookcase and a room divider.

Sottsass said. "It's not enough. Design should also be sensual and exciting."

Sottsass and his crew wanted to get away from the rationalism and monotony of the 1970s. Rationalism might make a decent chair, but it didn't stir the blood or charge the soul. Life had to be about something more than just 'functioning', right, otherwise why get out of bed in the morning?

We may as well live in sterile white cubes, sucking down flavourless nutrient smoothies. "Design is a way of discussing life," Sottsass would say. "It's a way of discussing society, politics, eroticism, food, and even design itself."

That last bit is important, because if nothing else, Memphis Milano generated a lot of chatter in the art world about what design *meant*, what its limits were, and who got to make those sorts of calls. Memphis didn't exist in a cultural vacuum, of course. Sottsass himself had been pushing boundaries since the 1950s, and 1980s postmodernism has the fingerprints of Art Deco and 1960s Radical Design all over it. But still, there was a difference.

Radical Design was (largely) a conceptual and countercultural movement, often focussing on utopian ideals rather than functional or commercial objects, i.e. stuff you could run out and buy. Its heroes were experimental groups like Archigram, Superstudio and Gruppo Strum[1].

Memphis Postmodernism had some of that same fuck-you spirit, sure, but it also added to the mix: playfulness, whimsy, irony and the exuberance of everyday things. It was antagonistic, but also straight-up fun. There was a kind of childlike glee with which Memphis designers tore up the rulebook (then turned the scraps into colourful, avant-garde lampshades).

Most importantly, the collective somehow balanced all that high-brow, art-wank theory with commercial success. The Memphis crew weren't just artists, they were *designers*. They made things you could use. And pretty soon their furniture, textiles, chairs and bookshelves started appearing in affluent houses all over the world. David Bowie became an avid collector. So did Karl Lagerfeld and Mick Jagger. The style tended to jive with anarchists and revolutionaries, and confuse – or mightily piss off – everyone else.

Although it only existed for seven years – Sottsass left in 1985 to try his hand at architecture, and the group technically disbanded in 1987 – Memphis would come to define the postmodern design movement. And maybe the next 40 years beyond that. A weird technicolour star that burned brightly, then flamed out. But that didn't really bother Sottsass. "Strong ideas are short-lived," he said once, "and it is not possible to develop them further."

Grandpa died last week
And now he's buried in the rocks,
But everybody still talks about
How badly they were shocked.
But me, I expected it to happen
I knew he'd lost control
When he built a fire on Main Street
And shot it full of holes.

Bob Dylan

It's kind of funny that one of the 20th century's most surreal, playful and individualist design movements was started by Sottsass, who fought for Mussolini as a militant member of the Italian Republican Fascist Party. But maybe that wasn't a coincidence. Sottsass didn't fight with the fascists by choice, after all; he was conscripted.

"After a happy youth in the mountains and a much less happy youth in various schools I got an architectural degree at the Turin Politecnico in 1939," he said. "I was then forced to waste seven years of my life in the army.

---

1 Archigram, Superstudio and Gruppo Strum were like the psychedelic rock stars of 1960s architecture and design. From futuristic 'walking cities' to cities without buildings at all – these collectives helped articulate a very different, very weird design language, which paved the way for groups like Memphis.

Tahiti – another masterpiece designed by Ettore Sottsass – is an "ironic zoomorphic lamp that resembles a toy". The base in black and white laminate (featuring Sottsass's 'Bacterio' pattern) supports a yellow stem underscored by a black foot, which support the round pink 'head' with its red 'beak'. The beak can be rotated to focus light in the desired direction.

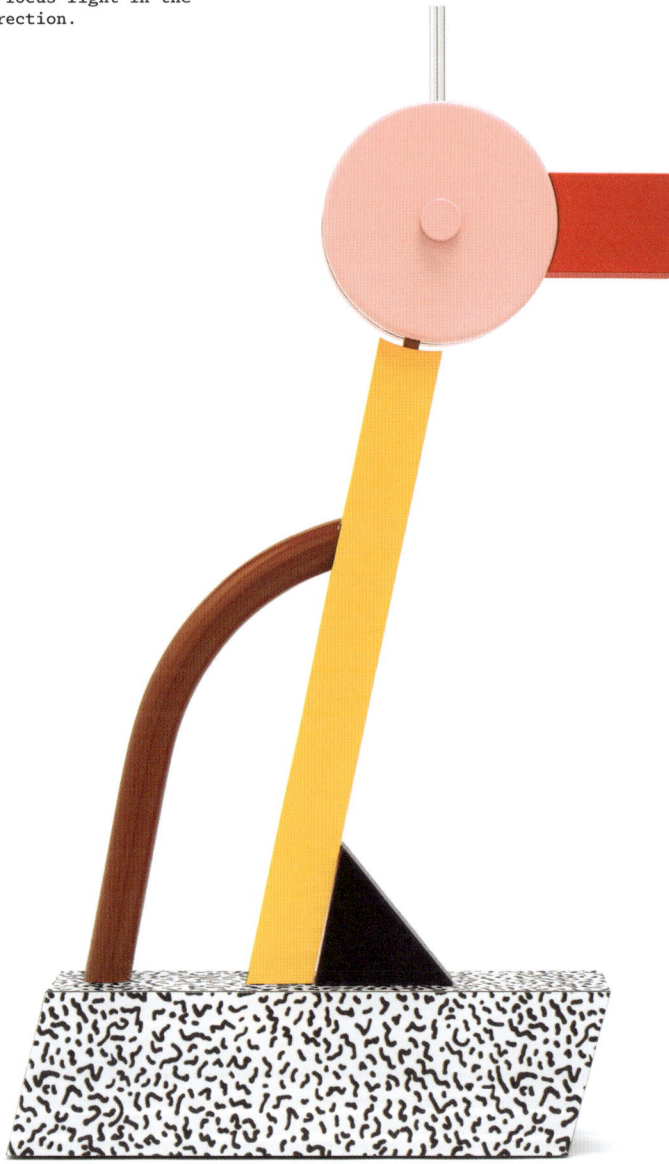

(Left)

arrot was designed by Nathalie Du Pasquier in 1985. The hand painted blue ceramic vase features two bands of decorative decals that are "sublimated" in the kiln.

(Below)

First is a sculptural chair designed by Michele De Lucchi in 1983. The metal frame is embellished with lacquered wood details including a blue adjustable back and two black spheres for armrests.

(Below)

It's hard to imagine a more apt representation for designer Peter Shire's work than *Big Sur* (1986). Shire described it thus: "Imagine throwing geometric objects into the air, allowing them to magically come together."

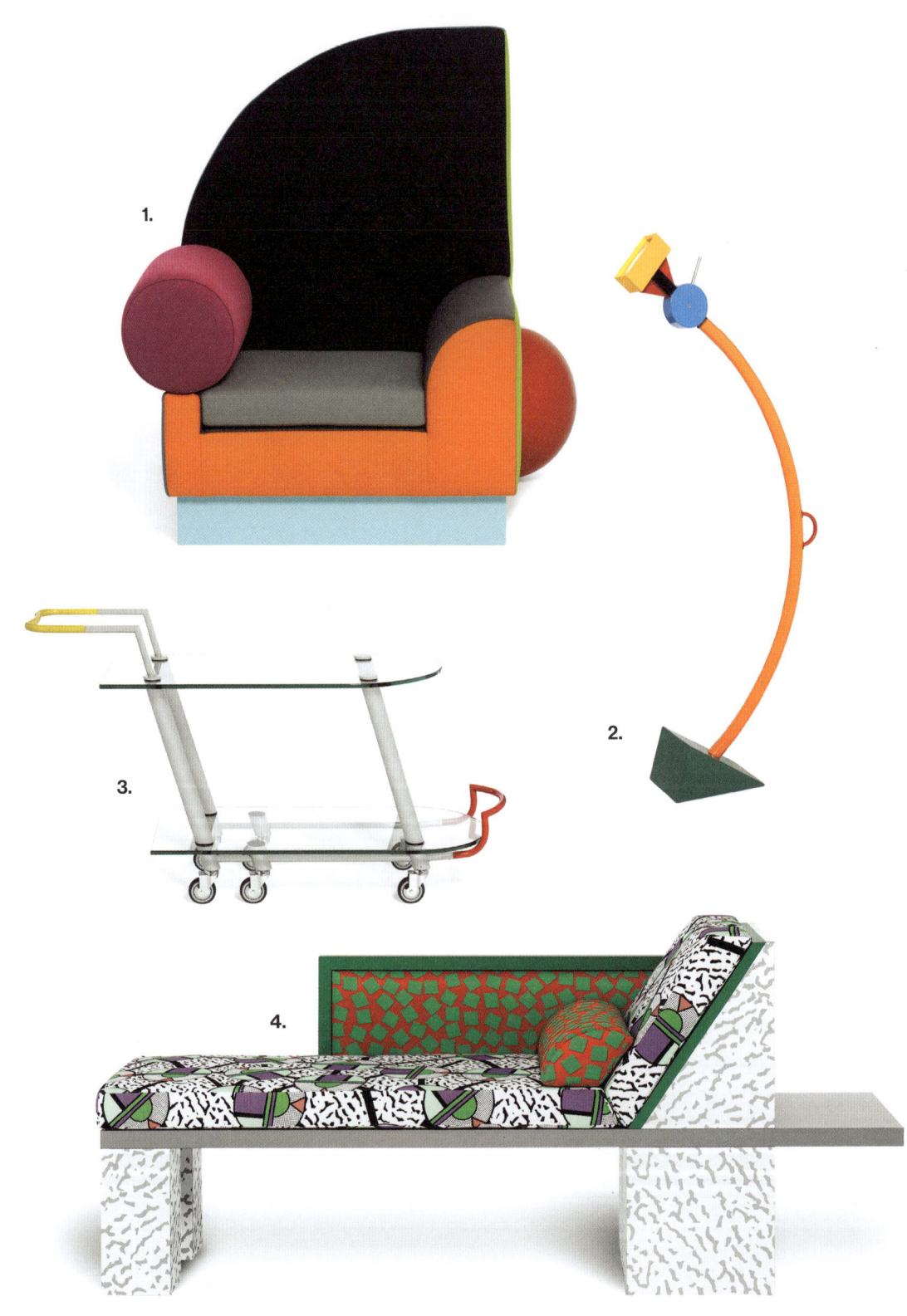

1.
2.
3.
4.

In a way, Sottsass' entire artistic philosophy can be read as a hardcore rejection of everything fascism stands for: Sottsass was global, not nationalist, curious, not threatened by curiosity, diverse and welcoming, rather than rigidly uniform. In fact, he hated uniformity. And that's another thing about 'Memphis style'; while the collective definitely had a *look* – think geometric shapes, bold, clashing colours, squiggles, checkerboards and other eye-watering patterns, plus the use of unconventional materials like laminate and plastic – every member of the group was encouraged to do their own thing.

That's why Sottsass' famous Carlton Room Divider, which turned the traditional bookshelf into some sort of many-armed Art Deco fertility idol, can sit comfortably alongside Peter Shire's Bel Air armchair, or a retina-blasting wooden chaise longue by George Sowden, or the iconic Memphis Tahiti lamp (another Sottsass de-construction, which looks like a duck that got lost and stumbled into a Picasso painting). Even when stuff gets surreal and weird, it's held together by a common thread.

"Memphis is not a style," said Italian design critic and Sottsass' wife, Barbara Radice, "Memphis is a way of being. A philosophy that plays with the possible and the impossible, the rational and the absurd."

Of course, not everyone saw it that way, and over the years Memphis has been labelled everything from a hot, kitschy mess to "a shotgun wedding between Bauhaus and Fischer-Price." As Pat Finn noted in *Architizer,* "These were designers who knew that to create a new visual language, one must be willing to create objects that are ugly. And to be sure, much of what this group created was brilliantly ugly." Emphasis on *brilliantly* there.

Memphis was a response to the perceived stasis of modernism, that feeling of everything staying the same, forever, like the make-believe world in Dylan's song; a nightmare of "going through all these things twice", where nothing grows or changes, and human beings are left to stagnate. That's the crisis that Memphis was trying to solve.

Of course, by the late 1990s, everyone was pretty sick of postmodernism (especially arts students who had to write dense, thesaurus-heavy essays on the topic) and the Memphis style had been relentlessly aped and smoothed-out and re-hashed, almost to death. It even inspired the visual language of 1990s Nickelodeon sets – all those 'brilliantly ugly' colours and food-splatter squiggle shapes. Postmodernism was old news. Bring on post-postmodernism.

Now the rainman gave me two cures
Then he said, "Jump right in".
The one was Texas medicine
The other was just railroad gin.
An' like a fool I mixed them
An' it strangled up my mind,
An' now people just get uglier
An' I have no sense of time.

Bob Dylan

Great art has this ability to be simultaneously timeless and of-its-time, and for a while there, people thought Memphis might fall only into the latter category. It's funny how quickly something radical can feel dated, even dorky.

1. The *Bel Air* chair by Peter Shire (1982) is another expression of the designer's interest in bold forms and colours and geometric shapes.

2. The *Treetops* lamp by Ettore Sottsass (1981) mimics a tall slender tree bending in the breeze with a bird at home in its upper branches.

3. The angled form of the *Hilton* trolley by Javier Mariscal (1981) gives the illusion of an object already on the move.

4. The *Royal* sofa-cum-chaise longue by Nathalie Du Pasquier (1983) features a collage of different Memphis fabrics (designed by George J. Sowden) that come together in "a shipwreck of the senses".

Over the years Memphis has been labelled everything from a hot, kitschy mess to "a shotgun wedding between Bauhaus and Fischer-Price." As Pat Finn noted in Architizer, "These were designers who knew that to create a new visual language, one must be willing to create objects that are ugly. And to be sure, much of what this group created was *brilliantly* ugly." Emphasis on brilliantly there.

The *Carlton* designed by Ettore Sottsass (1981).

MEMPHIS TODAY

After such an ephemeral existence, you might imagine production of all things Memphis halted when the group disbanded, and yet the brand's original collection has always remained in production. Now under the parent brand of Italian Radical Design – in good company with its fellow non-conformist design brand Gufram – we talk to the group's CEO Charley Vezza about Memphis in the modern day.

Why did it make sense for Italian Radical Design to take on the Memphis brand?

Italian Radical Design was founded with the mission of preserving and elevating Italian brands known for their unconventional approach to design. We began with Gufram and have since expanded to include three iconic brands – Gufram, Memphis and Meritalia® – each with a rich history and a strong creative identity.

Are there any particular efforts being made to honour the production methods of the original Memphis collection?

The original production methods have been carefully preserved, never altered or compromised. Memphis pieces continue to be crafted exactly as they were from the beginning, with only technical improvements being made where necessary, but always maintaining the integrity of their aesthetic. We also continuously explore ways to expand on the collective's ideas whilst staying true to their essence.

Does the transition from design collective to commercial brand sit a little at odds with the group's renegade values?

A common misconception is that Memphis started as a design collective and later became a brand. But in reality, Sottsass and his collaborators registered Memphis as a trademark and founded the company. What made Memphis revolutionary was not just its aesthetic but also its openness to new interpretations. I think Memphis remains relevant today as it continues to inspire us by offering new perspectives rather than fixed rules.

The Memphis archives are also an essential part of our work, as they help us to rediscover and add original designs to our catalogue. In bringing out these archival pieces, the pioneering spirit of Memphis continues to thrive, offering new generations of designers and collectors an ever-expanding world of radical possibilities.

Do you still have any interactions with any of the original members of the collective?

Yes, absolutely. We remain in close contact with the historical designers or their heirs; in particular with Barbara Radice, Ettore Sottsass's longtime partner and a key figure in shaping the Memphis vision.

memphis.it

Interview Eloïse Lachicorée

But the spirit of Memphis didn't die under the weight of 90s cynicism, and the 2010s saw a Memphis Renaissance, of sorts. In 2011, Christian Dior drew heavily from the Memphis school for the brand's Fall collection. In 2014, Nathalie Du Pasquier, one of the Memphis founding members, designed a collection of retro-graphic prints for American Apparel.

By the late 2010s, even mainstream commercial furniture brands like West Elm were dropping Memphis-inspired collections, and you can still see Sottsass' influence all over the place, from the pop-art designs of British artist, Camille Walala, to the more refined furniture of Milan's Studiopepe.

Memphis Milano is even indirectly responsible for 'Corporate Memphis', that classically blah and ubiquitous digital art style, in which colourful, faceless, wobbly-armed cartoon figures sell you everything from life insurance to apple juice. The Consumer Aesthetics Research Institute – an online Tower of Babel for everything design – describes Corporate Memphis as "The Generic 10s 'Friendly' Corporate Aesthetic, neo-Memphis, pastel colours, Mondrian influence, corporate appropriation of Vaporwave motifs, geometric sans typefaces, Monstera plants, exposed plywood, white walls, Matisse-influenced graphics." Trust us, you'll know it when you see it. Because you see it fucking everywhere.

But we do have to draw a line in the sand here. Corporate Memphis shares the name "Memphis", but that's about all it shares. Memphis Milano dabbled with the same saturated palette, but the bland commercialism and lazy sameness of Corporate Memphis would have annoyed Sottsass no end (if he hadn't died in 2007, aged 90).

There was nothing 'corporate' about Memphis Milano. In fact they were very famously and deliberately *anti*-corporate, along with anti-conservative, anti-mainstream, anti-boring, and anti-commercial for commercial's sake. Memphis became a consumer aesthetic, but right down at the core it was always more about the things money *can't* buy: creative freedom, radical individualism, joy, hope and the wonderful messiness of being human.

As Sottsass once said, "I am not interested in making a better thing. I am interested in making a different thing."

(Below)
George J. Sowden's *Pierre* (1981) is adorned in two clashing geometric patterns designed to enliven the table's rigid silhouette.

WORDS JAMES SHACKELL
IMAGES MARIA CLARA MACRÌ

THE HOME OF PHOTO SYNTH ESIS.

THE HOME OF ARCHITECTS **JULIE NEBOUT AND GIUSEPPE PUNZO** IS ALIVE WITH COLOUR AND CONTRADICTIONS. OLD AND NEW, REFINED AND RAW: THESE QUALITIES DON'T CLAMOUR FOR ATTENTION; THEY SING TOGETHER IN CAPTIVATING HARMONY. WELCOME TO THE LIGHT-FILLED NEAPOLITAN WORLD OF **LA FOTOSINTESI**.

Rising 150 metres over the cramped, warren-like streets of Naples, it's easy to see why the Bourbon kings[1] picked Capodimonte Hill as the location of their new hunting-lodge-slash-palace. From here you can see all the way east to the scooped-out shadow-peak of Mount Vesuvius, or south to the sparkling Gulf of Naples and distant Capris. When the early morning sun hits the city, Capodimonte Hill gets first dibs.

The gardens around Capodimonte are overgrown with orange and lemon trees, and in the evening twilight the smell of citrus floats through the district, carried gently on the breeze.

It was up here in 1738, on top of Capodimonte, that King Charles VII of Naples and Sicily built his Royal Palace, now a museum. The construction took over a century. Volcanic *piperno* rock was lugged all the way from quarries in Pianura, west of the city, and manicured gardens and hunting grounds, the Real Bosco di Capodimonte, sprouted on the hill.

But step away from the gardens and museums for a second – around a corner, down a crumbling side street, up several flights of nondescript stairs, through a door, and you'll find the light-filled apartment of architects and couple, Julie Nebout and Giuseppe Punzo – founders of the Italian design studio La Fotosintesi.

"We needed a home in Naples," Giuseppe says. "That's how the project began. Set on an old staircase, in a hilly area surrounded by gardens – it's a stark contrast to the bustling life of the city.

"We wanted to rediscover the beauty of *old* Neapolitan houses: the lofty ceilings, the dramatic light flooding the spaces, the traditional materials like vintage ceramics and tuff[2] stone walls."

The studio name – fotosintesi is Italian for *photosynthesis* – came about one appropriately sunny morning as Julie and Giuseppe were sitting on the balcony of their previous Neapolitan apartment. After two years in Paris, trapped in claustrophobic lockdowns, Naples felt like a breath of fresh air. Literally. The winds around this region are famous, part of local folklore: the warm sci-rocco, carried up from the Sahara, which makes the air feel heavy and people act funny; the icy *grecale*, blowing down from Greece; and the north-westerly *maestrale*, which often appears after storms, washing the sky clear and revealing the looming bulk of Mount Vesuvius.

On this day, however, both the sun and the espresso were strong and hot.

"One morning we were sitting on the balcony of our apartment, enjoying a radiant sunny day and good coffee," Julie says. "After all that time in lockdowns, we joked that we were literally doing our photosynthesis. We loved the idea, and we told ourselves that if we ever started an agency together, that would be the name."

The couple began hunting around for a more permanent base of operations, somewhere they could live, but also run the studio. Their search eventually led to Capodimonte and the historic Vico Paradisiello complex (translation: *paradise*), where they found a pint-sized apartment for sale. Space: small. View: to die for.

Measuring just 60 square metres, Julie and Giuseppe's 'paradise' is proof that creativity thrives on limitations, and you don't need a big space to accommodate big ideas. When the couple moved in, their first task was stripping back decades of, shall we say, 'courageous' design choices, revealing bare bones and a wonderfully un-blank slate.

1 The Bourbons rolled into southern Italy in 1734, when Charles of Bourbon (a Spanish prince) kicked the Austrians out and declared himself King of Naples and Sicily. Unlike your average absentee monarch, Charles actually cared about Naples, modernising the city and leaving a pretty sweet legacy before heading off to become King of Spain in 1759.

2 To the untrained eye, tuff looks like exposed concrete, but to the eye with brains filled with the right brand of knowledge it's actually made from ash ejected during a volcanic eruption, lithified and pressed into solid stone. There's something kind of magic about Naples in that way: construction from destruction, a city literally built from the ashes.

Julie Nebout and Giuseppe Punzo in their home, *Paradisiello* in Naples.

"The biggest design challenge was bringing back the apartment's historical elements," Giuseppe says.

"Over the years, various modifications had removed or concealed the original features. For example, we rediscovered the old colour palettes hidden behind layers of wallpaper. The dominant colours in the living room and bedroom are actually the original ones, which we then paired with contemporary elements to create a balanced contrast." More on this art form later.

It wasn't an easy build. Julie and Giuseppe were drawn to the apartment's cavernous Neapolitan ceilings and sweeping vista – from the living room, you can literally turn your head and see Mount Vesuvius. But the tiny floor plan required five re-drafts to get right, until, as Julie says, "every square centimetre was optimised".

That included an ingenious chartreuse mezzanine level, perched above the kitchen, which now functions as the couple's home-office-slash-design-studio. If you can't build outwards, build upwards, right? Further challenges came in the shape of the building's ancient, narrow stairs, which made transporting materials a real pain. "The construction company actually wanted to use a donkey to carry everything up here," Giuseppe laughs.

But when Julie and Giuseppe started stripping back layers, digging through the strata like archaeologists in the Quarry of Altamura, they discovered buried treasure. Some of the original Vietri floor tiles were still there, beautifully preserved, as were the walls, hewn from volcanic tuff rock.

(Top right)
Julie calls their style "joyfully eclectic". Despite representing 200-odd years of design, every element somehow flows together into a cohesive mishmash of shapes, styles and textures in Paradisiello.

(Bottom left)
During their renovations, Julie and Giuseppe discovered buried treasure: some of the original Vietri floor tiles were still there, beautifully preserved.

"We love the entrance in particular," Julie says, "with its vaulted ceiling, generous size, and just its sheer volume. It creates a sense of space as soon as you step into the apartment.

"The bedroom is another highlight, especially in the morning. During the renovation we actually discovered a heart carved into the wall, underneath the wallpaper. It's a symbol that was traditionally used to bring luck and protection to the inhabitants, so we decided to leave it in place."

Julie and Giuseppe planned their new home with care. Given their studio name, it's no surprise they wanted light to be a central feature, energising every room with shafts of gold. But the broader philosophy was to somehow mash classical Neapolitan design with modern materials: playful peach stairs leading up to the mezzanine, resin flooring, sculptural glass tables, and a galley kitchen decked out in mod-black and stainless steel.

The end result is what you might call 'eclectic', but not in a scattershot, throw-stuff-and-see-what-sticks sort of way. Julie calls it *"joyfully eclectic"* in that every single piece sparks joy, and their collective joy-sparking powers are enhanced by proximity to one another. Even when the designs don't match.

And it works, too. Despite representing 200-odd years of design, every element somehow flows together into a cohesive mishmash of shapes, styles and textures. Shades of red, grey, green and yellow dominate the space. Some walls are painted and rendered, others are left bare, or deliberately half-finished. It's Old Italy meets New, vintage chic meets 60s modernism, all bathed in that wonderfully soft, diffused Naples light.

"Naples is a beautiful yet fragile city, built in layers," Giuseppe says, "a millennia-old place where different eras coexist in what seems like chaos. We brought that same spirit into the project by respecting the existing layers of the space."

***

Here's a typical day inside Julie and Giuseppe's apartment. It starts with Giuseppe making coffee and bringing it to Julie in bed. The shutters are thrown back and light spills into the room. Then it's work time. Julie heads up the narrow stairs to the mezzanine and Giuseppe heads to the construction site to check progress on the latest build.

Naples is a beautiful yet fragile city, built in layers – a millennia-old place where different eras coexist in what seems like chaos. *We brought that same spirit into the project by respecting the existing layers of the space.*

Photo by Maria Clara Macrì, Paradisiello, Naples (2025).

Photo by Maria Clara Macrì, Paradisiello, Naples (2025).

The couple are a good team: Julie thrives on design, while Giuseppe handles execution. Lunch is a typical Neapolitan snack, maybe pasta and chickpeas, followed by meetings all afternoon. At dusk, as the setting sun turns Vesuvius purple, the couple go out for dinner, or stay home and watch a movie.

"Giuseppe is definitely the clean freak," Julie laughs. "He also has a great sense of humor and is very sensible and creative. But he's more cynical, discreet and introverted than I am."

"Yeah, Julie is definitely the fun and creative one," Giuseppe says. "I'm much more of a perfectionist. We usually decide everything together, although Julie has more control over design decisions."

With their own home, the couple decided to stick with French or local Italian designers, where possible[3]. They've also picked pieces you wouldn't necessarily expect. The cushions and upholstery, for example, are from In Casa by Paboy – a Naples-based collective founded by Gambian craftsman and designer Paboy Bojang, which offers safe work for refugees and migrants. Julie's always been a big fan of Charlotte Perriand, Carlo Scarpa and Tobia Scarpa – all that functional elegance and material mastery – whereas Giuseppe loves the pure lines of Italian rationalism. Think Giuseppe Terragni, or the Swiss-born Mario Botta.

Julie says they've made a conscious effort not to "give in to trends", but rather fill the space with stuff they like, both vintage and modern, in order to generate "unexpected encounters". Which is actually pretty good advice for us all. The whole apartment is really a masterclass in balancing contrasts, which Giuseppe admits is sometimes harder than it looks.

"All the elements need to be in harmony with each other; even the contrast must be harmonious. If there's a clear contrast, then we highlight it in a way that draws attention to that particular point. There's no secret – it's all about achieving harmony between the elements."

3 Julie is from Montmartre originally, whereas Giuseppe is Italian, so there's a definite Franco-Italian vibe running through the apartment. The couple actually met in Paris, while working for an architecture studio.

(Right)
"The bedroom is another highlight, especially in the morning," says Julie.

> How do you know when your clashing elements are "in harmony" and when they're just plain clashing? Well, that comes with experience, and maybe surrounding yourself with some brutally honest friends.

But it also helps to have a 'look', or even a feeling, in mind. Julie says every La Fotosintesi job aims to create an interior that "already feels lived in". Not a sterile showcase or wanky thought experiment, but a living, breathing, crumb-strewn world. A home, in other words, not just a house.

"That's what I love about this space," she says. "It evolves throughout the day. It feels alive. My favourite moment is in the morning, when it's bathed in light, offering a breathtaking view of the gardens full of lemon trees, Mount Vesuvius, Naples and the sea.

"The volumes, the colours – I love everything about this space. It's where our thoughts and souls find peace."

Project: Poerio/cabinet de curiosités
Design: La Fotosintesi
Size: 70 sqm/753 sqft
Location: Naples, Italy

INTERVIEW ELOÏSE LACHICORÉE
IMAGES CARLO ORIENTE

A passion for antique collecting and the colour brown are things that, in the wrong hands, could make a home feel quite drab and antiquated. But tucked away on a narrow cobblestone street in Naples' Chiaia district, is an apartment where both are harmoniously combined and contrasted to create an elegant, characterful *cabinet de curiosités* of a home. With a striking colour palette inspired by the city's rich history – from its royal past, to its surrounding natural beauty and the sea; the rooms in *Poerio* communicate with one another through the pairing and contrast of intense and cooler colours, each with its own soul that harmonises with the carefully selected furnishings and finishes. The complete redesign of this apartment was a close collaboration between architects Giuseppe Punzo and Julie Nebout – co-founders of La Fotosintesi – and their clients; with the final result being a unique, bold and light-filled Neapolitan home.

Tell us a bit about your clients ... clearly some interesting characters live here ...

Nicola and Chicco are a creative, open-minded couple who are both passionate about refined Italian and Swedish design from the 1940s, 50s and 60s. This is actually the second project we have worked on with them so we knew they had a preference for darker spaces, that brown was Nicola's favourite colour and that they preferred interiors with significant character. Their tastes played a large role in the design of the space, which we definitely learnt a lot about!

How did the desire to use the space for both living and working shape your vision for the project?

Nicola, who's a doctor, wanted to use the space as both a medical practice and a private living space, which definitely influenced the design and ultimately shaped our vision for the project. It gave us additional opportunities to create more varied environments within the same design though, making the project more intricate and diverse. *Poerio* also isn't the clients' permanent residence either, so we had to design a space equipped with the necessary living essentials of a home without treating it too much like a main residence.

Talk us through the design phase of the project. Were you given a lot of creative freedom? Was it a close collaboration?

The preliminary project was carried out in several steps: first, we needed to understand the tastes and the vision of our clients. Following various interesting meetings where we discussed the project, and art and design more generally, we were able to interpret their way of envisioning the space. From there, it was a very close collaboration throughout all the phases of design and construction – even down to the painting of every single piece of furniture. The only real constraint we faced on this project was around the set-up and structure of the medical practice.

(Page 62)
Julie Nebout and Giuseppe Punzo of La Fotosintesi in *Poerio* - designed for their clients, Nicola and Chicco.

(Right)
The apartment's living space doubles as a waiting room. The light-filled and ornately decorated room features a 1920s Florentine chandelier and a pair of sofas designed by Göran Malmvall from the 1940s.

In which ways is this project different from the others you've worked on?

This project was different because it was a real journey with two clients who were very involved in the process and had a clear vision for the design right from the beginning, whilst also giving us the freedom to use our imagination. It was also an exchange as well as a journey, in the sense that they taught us so much about vintage Italian and Swedish design.

Can you tell us the story behind choosing the name *Poerio*?

> We took inspiration from the name of the street where the studio is located – *Poerio*. The idea behind the secondary name *cabinet de curiosités* came from our clients' passion for collecting objects from different design eras, which, when well arranged, create an interesting eclectic harmony.

The cabinet in the medical office where lots of these objects are stored is a real treasure trove, but the whole apartment itself is a real *cabinet de curiosités* with different objects and trinkets from their collection showcased throughout.

Which features of the space have been designed to transition between home and working life?

Whilst the primary function of the downstairs space serves as part of the medical practice, the entrance and waiting room have been designed to seamlessly transition between home and working life. The entrance hall in *Poerio* is not only important when used as a reception area, but also in a domestic setting. We always try to integrate an entry area as the first filter between the street and the home itself, making for a clear transition between the outside world and domestic setting. The waiting room, which has two sofas, can be used as a comfortable living room where one can read a book or watch a movie after work. The metal staircase leading to the mezzanine, on the other hand, creates a clear distinction rather than a transition between the working and private living spaces.

The cabinet located in the medical office houses much of Nicola and Chicco's personal antique collection – a *Cabinet de Curiosités*.

How did you and your client approach the element of colour in this design? How was the colour palette conceived?

Poerio's colour palette is the result of envisioning an internal journey through each of the spaces in the studio. Starting with the apartment's entrance and waiting room – pastel and muted shades of blue, brown and red are found, creating a more subdued, serene and calm atmosphere. Following through to the corridor connecting the waiting room to the doctor's office is an intentionally more intense space thanks to the lower ceiling paired with darker shades of brown and dimmer lighting. Finally reaching the doctor's office: opening out into a double-height ceiling, open space with deeper shades of blue helping to cool down the intense red. The play of colour, light and varying heights is the real soul of the project. The central brown part of the studio was then designed as a 'box within a box', creating a certain depth within this central section.

The pairing and layering of bold colours is quite unconventional but work harmoniously to create depth and character. Did you have any reservations when approaching such bold use of colour?

No! We truly believe that a house should reflect the sensations that the client wants to bring into and experience in their home. Colour has the power to do this from the different feelings and moods it can evoke in each of us. In *Poerio*, we played around a lot with contrast, choosing colours that respond well to each other, and aligned with our clients' vision and the atmosphere they wanted to create through the design. We use a lot of colour in our work in general, both in the interiors and furnishing. We think it's one of the most important elements of a project. So we don't shy away from injecting colour wherever we can!

(Left)

A more subdued palette of muted shades of blue, brown and red appear in the apartment's entrance area before increasing in intensity further into its other rooms.

(Above)

Not your regular doctor's office.

(Top left)
While blues, browns and reds are a common thread throughout the colour scheme, each space has its own distinct palette, including the powder room accessed via a sliding door off the kitchen.

(Bottom right)
Poerio's brown bathroom features brass brutalist wall lamps by Danish designer Svend Aage Holm Sørensen in the 1960s.

(Right page)
The kitchen, an essential part of Nicola and Chicco's secondary residence, comprises of rich wooden joinery, a set of stools from Tom Dixon's 1980s *Banana Chair* series for Cappellini, and a 1970s style painted metal pendant light.

SMALL HOMES — POERIO

VIA GIULIO PETRA

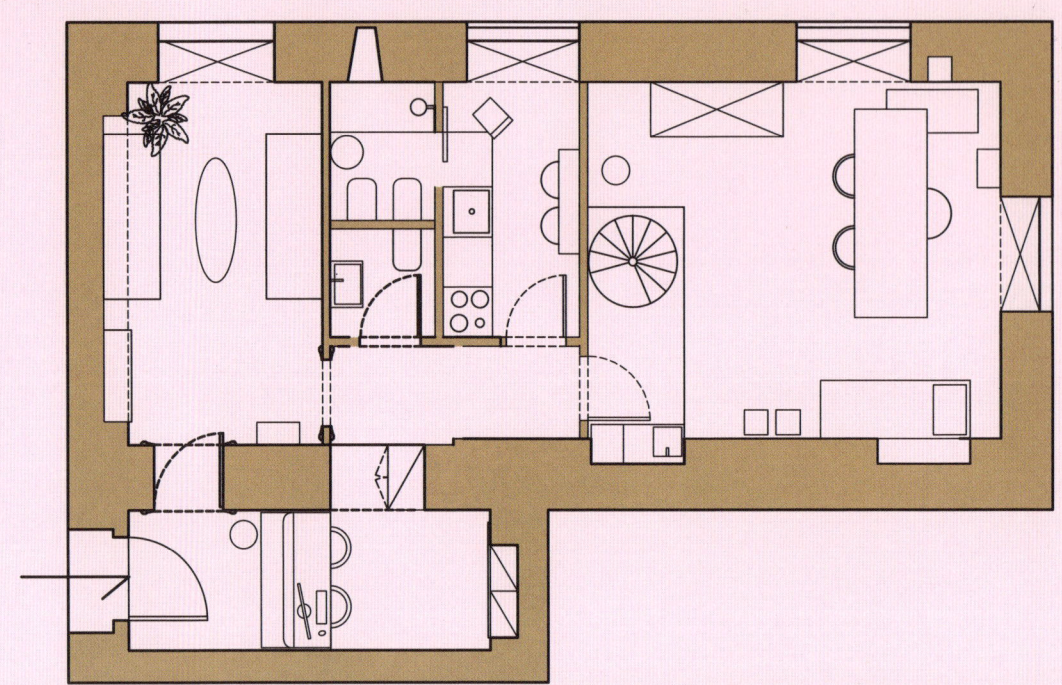

VIA GIULIO PETRA

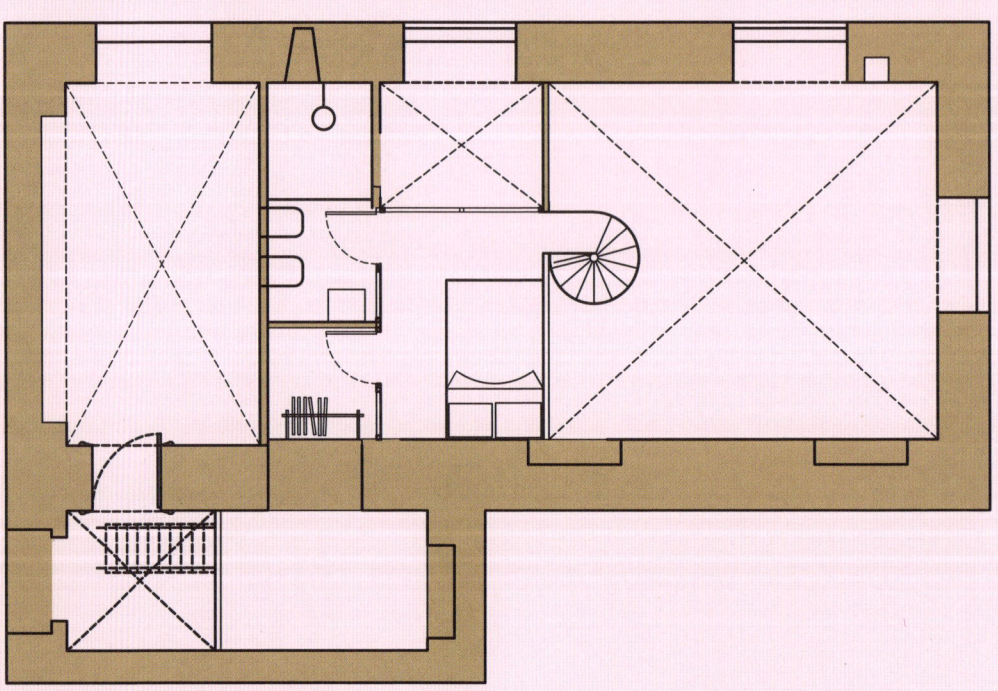

The red metal spiral staircase is one of Poerio's most striking features, connecting the lower level of the apartment to its mezzanine. The staircase offers a clear division between the medical practice space below and the private domain of the mezzanine level.

What defined your approach to colour in this design?

Definitely playing around with and being more daring with colour – pairing bold shades without disrupting the harmony of the space. Also exploring how colours and different materials such as wood, metal and marble can work together and complement each other. We also used colour to create a story within the studio and between the different rooms and spaces.

Collaborating with other artisans and creatives seems to play a big part in your design ethos. Tell us more …

One of the most important elements of our work is our collaboration with artisans and craftsmen who bring a very high level of expertise, creativity and individuality to their designs. We're fortunate enough to have worked with artisans who have allowed us to experiment with new materials in order to bring our ideas to life and help find the right balance within a project. Various custom-made furniture pieces featured in *Poerio* are examples of these kinds of collaborations.

(Top)

The porthole (one of Julie and Giuseppe's favourite features of Poerio) opens out to connect the bedroom and mezzanine level with the floor below.

Are there any colours you'd like to explore further and experiment with in the future?

We went through a long orange phase, then there was also a Pompeian red with blue phase. We're currently really into burgundy, paired with antique pink, sienna, terracotta or khaki green. There was also a period of time where we were into more vibrant colours, but we'd say we're now more into using slightly more muted tones.

For each of you, what are your favourite details or spaces within this design?

Guiseppe: I love the way the different layers or volumes of the space seamlessly fit together. I also like that the mezzanine level creates space for the double height ceiling in the kitchen below. Although there's a clear distinction between the two levels in the studio, I love how the porthole in the bedroom connects with the floor below.

Julie: I agree, I also love the bedroom porthole up on the mezzanine and, of course, the metal staircase that leads up to the mezzanine. But beyond that, the colour tones throughout the project are my favourite element. The bathrooms are another favourite too. I think that the design and styling of the entire space is very unique which really reflects our clients' personality; that's something really special about *Poerio* – there's no other apartment quite like theirs.

Project: Pine
Design: Nicholas Gurney
Size: 55 sqm/592 sqft
Location: Sydney, Australia

INTERVIEW ELIZABETH PRICE
IMAGES MICHAEL WEE

Nicholas Gurney found his way to his clients for this project the way many of the best designers do – through friendship. This perhaps explains the warmth with which he introduces Pine on his website: "Shining brightly with vivacity and wit. Years of yearning unremembered." The "years of yearning" refers to the years that his clients, Vicki Papageorgopoulos and Kirthana Selvaraj longed for a more open space that better responded to their way of living. The interventions that took place in their apartment in Sydney's inner west to satiate this yearning were not drastic but are hardworking solutions all the same. They carry all the hallmarks of Nicholas's talents for inspired spatial organisation and clever custom furniture solutions that respond so intuitively to our more relaxed modes of contemporary living. And so, with the years of yearning behind them, this is finally a home where the "vivacity and wit" of Pine's residents can shine bright.

This is such a charming and characterful home. Who are the charming characters who live here?

Nicholas: Kirthana and Vicki both have a great sense of humour and a strong social justice lens in all that they do. Kirthana is an artist and academic and Vicki works in community development. They love art, making art, collecting art, enjoying music and the theatre. They especially love travelling and eating, and they love living in the inner west and their cute dog-park family made of neighbours and furry friends.

How did you all meet? And how did you come to be involved in reimagining their home?

Nicholas: The link dates back more than 10 years to one of my earliest projects. In 2014, I undertook a project – Kanimbla Hall – that then led to another for that client's friend. That client's friend was Grant and the project was The Warren. Vicki and Grant are pretty much besties. Needless to say, I'm glad I did a good job on that one and so got this gig.

Ah, The Warren … One of our all-time favourites[1]. But back to this gorgeous place: tell us about the original apartment and the building it's in … What prompted the reno?

Vicki: We wanted to open up the space – we felt too closed in with the previous layout. We didn't have much storage space, and we wanted to update the kitchen and bathroom too. We wanted to live as big as we could in a smaller space and needed the design to get us there.

Nicholas: Vicki is forgetting one of the primary reno prompts – a pet-friendly (wee-tolerant) floor.

Okay, we'll come back to the wee-tolerant floor. What was the approach to solving the space and storage issues?

Nicholas: The first hurdle and most obvious manoeuvre was to remove the wall that separated the kitchen and laundry and the kitchen/diner from the living space. Vicki had agonised over its presence (and yearned for its disappearance) for years. By default, a dining spot would have been created by removing the wall, but it felt too simplistic.

(Top and bottom/Right)
The "floating bench and dining combo" in action.

> I wanted to promote an effortless circulation and double-down on their desire for openness. The result being the floating bench and dining table combo. I like playing into the realities of how we live nowadays, where dining tables are used sometimes rather than all the time. The bulk of the kitchen and laundry was then pushed to the flanks, which allowed us to overlap with and fulfil storage requirements.

What were the non-negotiables in the design?

Vicki: Trying to make as much floor space available and to bring both intentional and functional design into our little home.

Nicholas: And the wee-friendly floor. Vicki also had to have some terrazzo. So we stuck some in the bathroom.

There's that wee-tolerant floor again… Tell us about your dog and what you all love to do at home. What kind of life do you lead within these walls?

Kirthana: Our dog Oscar now lives with Vicki's mum because he has doggy dementia and was getting stressed in the small space. He is now enjoying a big backyard. The apartment felt weird without a dog so we added a puppy to the family – Bernie – who enjoys running around the apartment.

---

1 This fabulous 49sqm Sydney apartment featuring a distinctive golden mirror-clad central pod appeared on Never Too Small's YouTube channel in 2019 and continues to be a major audience (and team) favourite. It also featured in our first book, *Reimagining Small Space Living*.

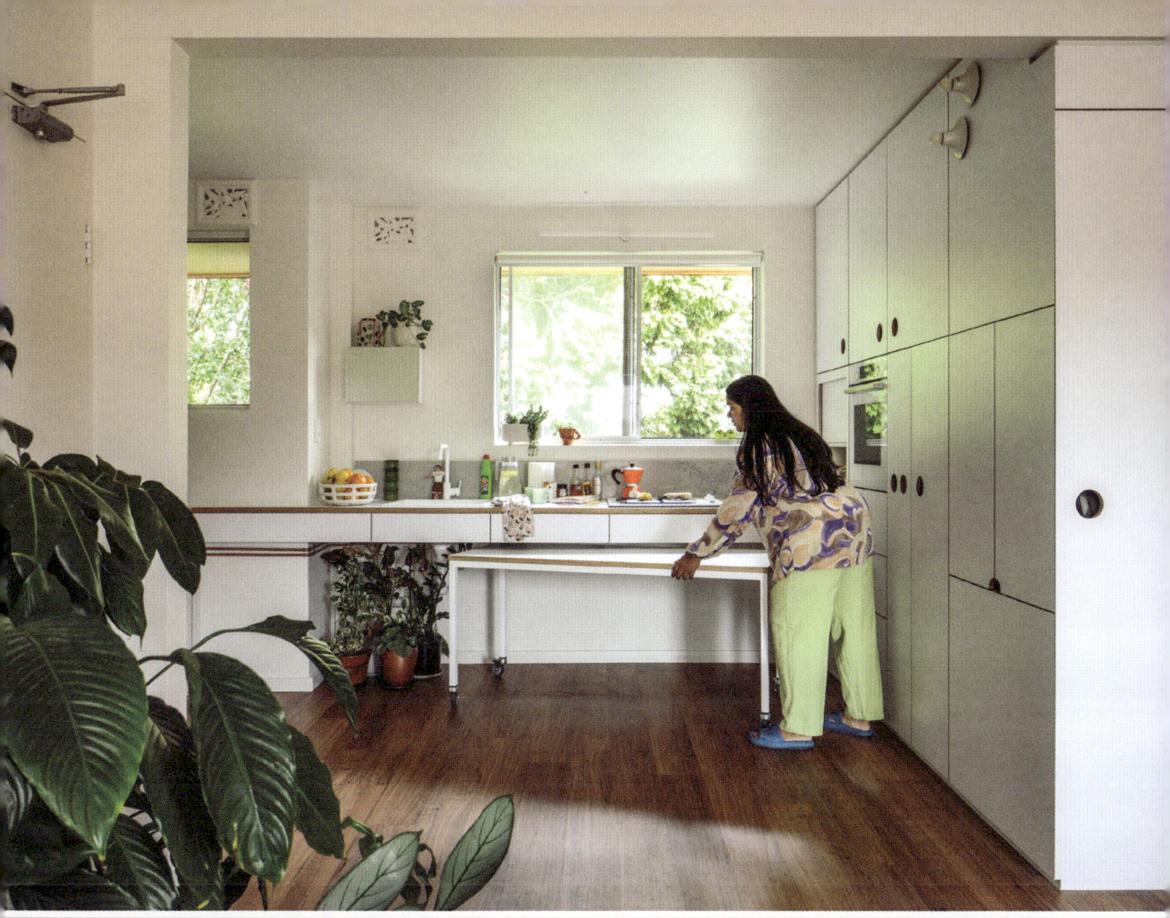

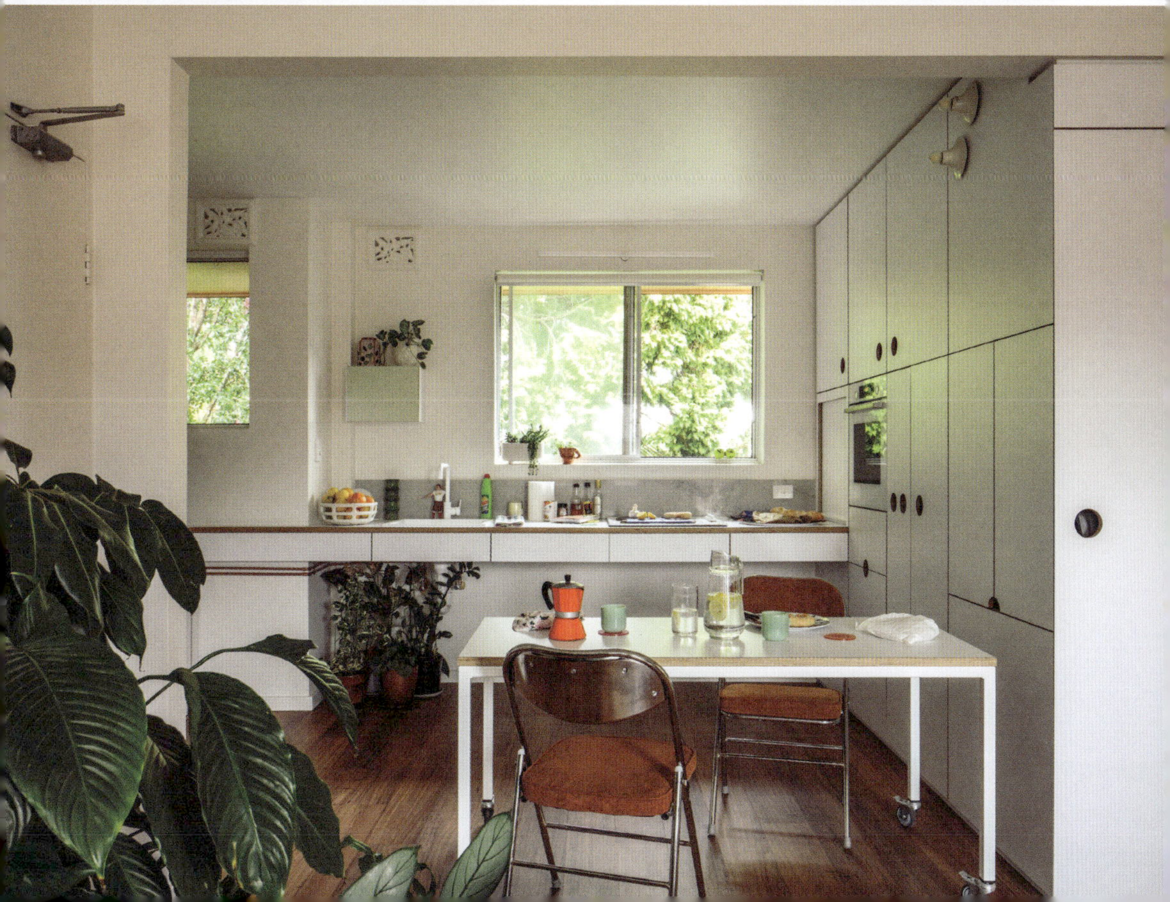

SMALL HOMES

PINE

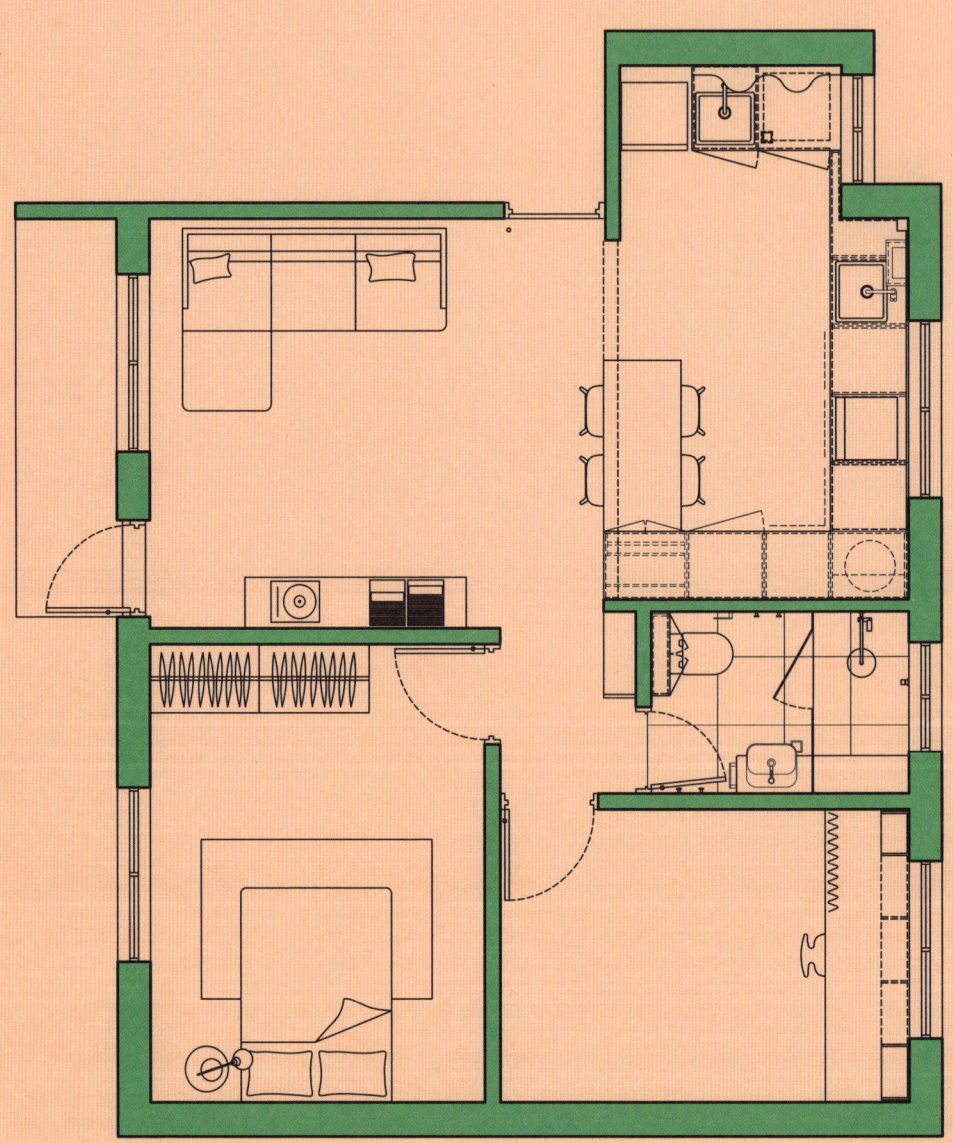

Vicki: Kirthana works from home so the study and the table on wheels in the kitchen come in handy. We spend most of our time in the lounge room as we love listening to music and watching films. Kirthana loves cooking too, so the larger kitchen and pullout pantry that houses her favourite spices are welcome additions. We also love pulling out a book from the window library if only just to admire all the spines. (I'm aware that sounds weird).

What kinds of questions did you ask Vicki and Kirthana to nut out your response to their brief, Nic?

Nicholas: I don't have to ask a lot of questions when people are honest and transparent about what and why. There was never any suggestion that this was a stepping stone for Vicki and Kirthana. It was simultaneously a project with a very concise brief and enough wiggle room to explore some tailored solutions.

Talk us through the choices of materials throughout and why these choices were made …

Nicholas: Vicki will tell you in no uncertain term that things have to be hard-wearing and easy to clean. We started with the floor and found the best possible option. The chestnut coloured timber was not what any of us had in mind but it was the pick of the bunch. It both paired and contrasted nicely with white, and we knew that plants and art would do a lot of the heavy lifting with respect to ambience. Targeted use of marble and terrazzo satisfied Vicki's "need for some stone". For high touch points, the white laminate is adhered to plywood.

Yep. The colour palette really allows Vicki and Kirthana's beautiful and colourful artwork to pop. So this idea for the plants and art to do "the heavy lifting" on the ambience side was always the plan from the start?

Nicholas: Yes. As much as Vicki loved what we'd done at Grant's place, something with a little more restraint was preferred.

(Top left)
As Kirthana loves cooking the pull-out pantry "that houses her favourite spices" is a favourite feature.

(Top right)
The pull-out dining table often Kirthana's base when she works from home.

The custom media unit in the living room features bespoke storage for the couple's vinyl collection and amp and a pull-out coffee table. These photos were taken back in the days before dear Bernie moved to Vicki's mum's house.

PINE SMALL HOMES

"Vicki also had to have some terrazzo. So we stuck some in the bathroom."

The bookcase framing the window: it's such a hardworking and attractive storage solution. Is this an approach you've used before or did it emerge as part of this project?

Nicholas: We wanted to fashion some storage without compromising the opportunity for the studio to be converted to a second bedroom if needed. I have used a similar tactic in the past, whereby a white shroud frames the window and magnifies the intensity of the natural light. The view outside to the neighbouring buildings (and likely a future development site) was not a favourite. As such, the bookcase encourages eyes to linger inside instead.

The clever slide-away coffee table and kitchen table are such simple but effective solutions too. We've seen this move from Nic before, but was this something you requested from his previous work, Vicki? Or an approach that Nic brought to the table (ahem) himself?

Vicki: I'm not a fan of dining tables in smaller spaces as they take up too much space, so a table that could be rolled away when not in use was a very welcome solution. Kirthana loves a theatrical reveal and so tucking away the tables makes for some fun with guests, especially when they think they'll be eating off their laps.

(Left)

The bookcase was designed to encourage "eyes to linger inside". The painting is one of Kirthana's original artworks: *Mimz the magnificent* (2017).

How long did the renovations take? Was there a tight budget?

Nicholas: The renovation took 14 weeks to complete. And, yes. The budget was pretty darn tight.

How has the redesign altered the way you enjoy your home, Vicki?

Vicki: Everything we own has a place, which makes it easier to keep the apartment tidy. It also makes us appreciate what we do have and makes it clear what we don't in fact need for joy and comfort.

And if you had to name your favourite detail in the apartment?

Nicholas: The kitchen.

> It's a difficult space in which to reinvent the wheel. It's suitably functional and gifts the area it needn't occupy back to the space. The original relationship between kitchen and dining are reimagined but still intertwined.

Vicki: I love it all! I often find myself looking at different elements like the copper pipes under the kitchen bench. The cut out circles in the joinery, the curvy shelves, the bookshelf around the window in the second room. I really enjoy it all.

Kirthana: We love the little elements of humour, for example the boob lights in the kitchen. We also love the wavy shelves and the terrazzo tiles in the bathroom called 'Fatima's reflection'. A lot of reflection happens in there. And Bernie loves body-sliding across the pet-friendly floor with her toys.

Wild, Wild Colour

An interview with artist Kirthana Selvaraj.

INTERVIEW KIRSTEN DRYSDALE **IMAGES** ANNA KUCERA

Kirthana Selvaraj is someone who honours the full spectrum of the rainbow. Her studio in Sydney's inner west is stocked with every pigment you can imagine. Huge bold portraits lean against the walls in a visual chorus of reds, yellows, blues, browns, and splashes of pink, orange and teal. These colours have brought the Sydney-based artist plaudits, awards and, most importantly, joy. They bring others joy too: One of her best-known works – a painting celebrating the achievements of the Matildas – the Australian women's national football team – has just been transformed into a spectacular 57-metre-long immersive mural at Sydney's Olympic Stadium.

Kirthana's desk is littered with paint tubes – well-squeezed Viridian Green rolls around with Dioxazine Violet and Quinacridone Magenta. Sometimes, she has to travel halfway around the world to find the exact hue she's after.

"I went to Japan, and I found this incredible range of really fluorescent oil paints with really rich saturation. And I never can find that here in Australia. I picked up like 20 of them. They're so juicy – I just want to eat them!"

It's hard to choose a favourite, but Kirthana says she goes through more tubes of Cadmium Red and Indian Yellow paint than any other. (If you don't count Titanium White, which is a mixing medium, and that's a bit boring, so no, we won't count that.)

"You can probably see a lot of those colours [Cadmium Red and Indian Yellow] in my paintings. I'd say my favourite would be Indian Yellow. It's a little bit transparent, so I layer it like a glaze on top of a really vibrant acrylic ground underpainting," she says, walking over to a painting to show exactly where she has done just this. "You can kind of see here – where there's like a hot pink underneath, and I put Indian Yellow over the top and I smudge it out and it kind of looks like it's sort of fluorescent coming from underneath."

The painting does indeed seem to glow. It is, like all her works, quite literally vibrant.

"I think about what I use most and am always repurchasing, and it's always Indian Yellow. And it's not just because I'm Indian! It's the true, purest version of a yellow-orange hybrid that I find works well with all the tones I try to paint with."

Perfectly mixing pigments to get those precise tones, especially diverse skin tones, is a Kirthana specialty. This skill and many other aspects of her life – including her journey from biotechnology student to the art studio, being a triplet, and growing up in New Zealand – all feature in my conversation with artist Kirthana Selvaraj.

...

You've shared how difficult some artists – portrait painters in particular – seem to find painting the diversity of tones of brown skin. And it made me think of how when colour photography was first invented, the film stock was calibrated for white skin – Caucasian skin. And they even had this thing called 'the Shirley card' with a photograph of a white woman to set it to. Are there similar issues in the art world in terms of the paint stock you can buy?

I remember in 2013 I got a scholarship which was basically a whole bunch of oil paints. And I was curious about this one colour called 'Flesh Tone', and I was like "yeah, let's try that!". And I looked at it, and it was this sort of pinky-beige colour. And I remember thinking "oh okay, well, you just work with this and you mix different tones". But then I started getting a little bit annoyed that this was premixed to be this universal skin colour that isn't accurate. And when I see people painting brown skin, it's always so flat. It's like "okay, you mix a little bit of Burnt

Umber and you put a little bit of black and then a little bit of a white and there's 'brown skin'". But brown skin has all these nuances – when blood reaches the skin in certain brown skin, sometimes it looks a little bit deeper, or it looks a little bit more purple in the sunken areas. There's the highlights and the lilac tones, but also the shadows are a little bit green.

So often what I see is missing is all the depths of colours that I actually see in the world. And that's why I sort of exaggerate the colour that I see in my paintings. I amp it up, because for me that makes it feel more alive. It makes it feel like skin, like a living person.

Are you ever tempted to play around in a monochromatic way or is it rainbow all the way?

For the longest time I only worked in charcoal. So that was always just black. I never worked with colour – in terms of actually painting with colour, outside of being a child – until probably 2013. Before that I was working with dry mediums like charcoal, and I would grind that down and sort of 'paint' with it. I was more focused on form and volume and composition and shape. And I guess I was afraid of colour? I didn't know how to tame it. It felt wild, like a wild beast. But it was funny – when I first started using colour I was like: "I feel like I can breathe, like this feels like oxygen in my lungs!" So it's hard to think of going back. I can do a sort of more muted palette, with bursts of colour randomly underneath. But I don't know if I would ever go with a greyscale work where it's just gradients and shapes, and colour isn't informing the work in any way. It doesn't feel like me anymore.

So you were studying biotechnology before you became an artist – what's the story there?

I spent a year just at bars going what exactly am I doing here? In fact I think I was drunk for that first year! Honestly – I was a terrible student. But I'm from an immigrant culture, which is sort of like, 'well, even if it feels shit you just do it and we'll see the outcome later'. This yearning to get out of there was actually the only thing that comes to mind about my time there. It made me really see I can tick that off now, that's definitely not what I want to do. I feel that's a typical story from my cultural background, where we start on a path that's created for us by our parents or cultural pressures, and then we start to take on this sense of autonomy and discover our own sense of agency and what we actually want. So I felt like this was my chance to break that cycle, and find joy in what I do.

Has any of that scientific background influenced your art?

I think maybe just the discipline of it; having structure to the process of something, the discipline of getting up early and doing the work. I sometimes start my day at 5 or 6am, and I'm painting, and I see it as work and less than something that is just for fun and something that I love. It's something I'm determined to see as a part of my life that will sustain me, but also be a career.

(Right)
Details from Kirthana's studio space in Sydney including one of several portraits she has painted of artist, friend and mentor, Ramesh Mario Nithiyendran.

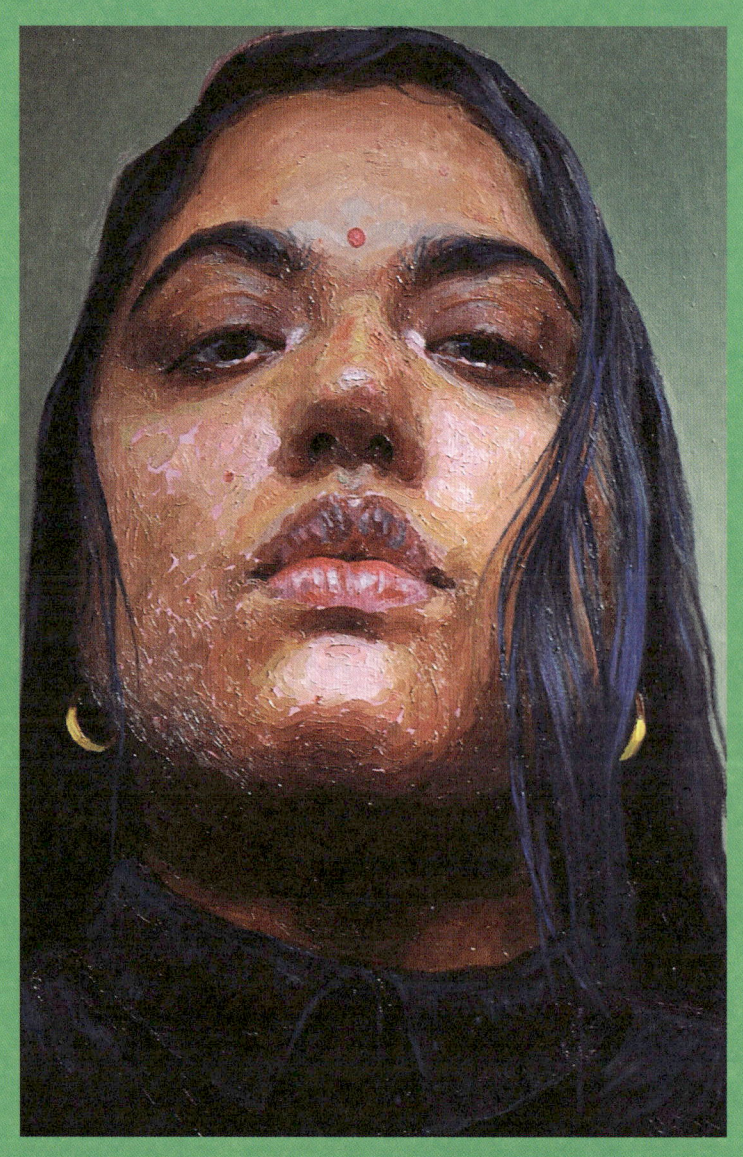

Kirthana's self portrait: *Kirthana*, 2020, oil on canvas.

<u>Speaking of what you don't want to do, you've also said art school was interesting less because you learned how to be an artist and more because you learned what you didn't want to be. Could you expand on that a little?</u>

When I was at art school, I felt that figurative painting was seen as this archaic relic that was laughed at. It was like, "painting's dead, it's outdated – do something contemporary". And I always used to think, 'well, what does that mean?' Because if we looked at figurative painting, often what we saw was certain bodies expressed, certain gazes, right? And for me it always felt to disrupt that or subvert that became more important in my practice, while still using this 'archaic' medium to convey that.

I think what I didn't want to be was an artist that listened to my lecturer solely, and an artist that tried and experimented and failed to then rediscover what they actually wanted to do.

At art school, lecturers had their own books of what contemporary art is and what has longevity and what will sustain your practice. I just wanted to discover the part of me that felt the most seen, and painting has always been something that I felt closest to and I didn't want to pretend I didn't love to paint.

<u>What is your earliest memory of creating art?</u>

Okay – I remember, and this is funny because it's this idea of 'augmenting reality', I suppose – because I was really young and I remember wanting to be a doctor. I think I was six, and I cut out cardboard shapes of a doctor's apron, and I put a cross on it and I got a hat. And I remember thinking there's so much power in making something, because then I can believe it's real. I just remember that thought, when I was very, very young. But when I first got into actually creating and painting I was probably nine, and I used to paint the deities in my parents' house, like Krishna. And I would always paint them very effeminate and my mum would always ask me about that. And even back then I just thought this sort of idea of gender expression felt really limiting, and I never really fully connected to that until this question actually, that you're now asking me. Because I used to always paint the deities in dresses and gowns. I'm just having a flashback now of when I was really young and feeling like I'm not getting it right. But actually it was probably something I've always felt, and now I'm kind of pursuing it more seriously.

<u>Do you still have any of those paintings?</u>

I don't have any, it's a bit sad actually – we got rid of so many of my drawings and paintings. But my parents kept this one drawing I did of Krishna with very long eyelashes! There was one painting I did that was of a tuatara [a type of reptile unique to New Zealand], and I got selected in my school to have my work in the Auckland Museum of Art, and I remember I was very young then and that's when I first thought "Oh, I think I'm good at this". But we didn't keep it.

<u>You've talked before about growing up feeling quite lonely, and I was wondering was that in the sense of not seeing people who looked like you represented much? Or were you a lonely child? What was your childhood like?</u>

God, that's a loaded question! What was my childhood like?

<u>I know – sorry. We're not in therapy. We don't have to go too deep!</u>

Well, I'm a triplet, actually. I've got a brother and sister my age.

<u>What?!</u>

I always forget to tell people that, because to me, that's normal. I'm like - oh, that's right, it's not really the usual! In so many ways, when you're a triplet, you want to be different and you want to feel unique. All our birthdays were shared, so you want to feel like there was something about you that was special, that wasn't shared. And I think the sense of loneliness came from not necessarily feeling like I knew who I was. Identity becomes sort of blurred when you're a three-person-unit, and you're navigating the world together but you think very differently. And also yeah, I did feel it was hard - I was born in New Zealand, and grew up in Auckland for about 10 years, then moved to Invercargill. That was particularly lonely because there were hardly any people of colour. I think we were one of two South Asian families in my town, and it was always about trying to acculturate or assimilate, whether that's how you look or how you sound, your accent, how you dress. And there was always this projection of this self that was never real. So I think loneliness stems from inauthenticity. And you know you're performing, there's a dissonance there because you know you're not being real. So I think the loneliness came from a disconnect between how I saw myself, and how I was perceived by others.

<u>And now here you are, proudly painting yourself, and people like you, every day. How have people responded to your artwork?</u>

I can only speak to those who have reached out to me - but I've had the loveliest messages from really young, queer South Asian people saying 'I feel seen!' and 'I feel like maybe I can hope for more for my career, thank you for representing'. But I don't see myself that way - I don't see myself as a role model or anything - I feel like anyone can be this person that does work that means something to them. It's persistence. There's no crazy formula. It's just being willing to fail and to not expect a perfect outcome. So I really hope to see more South Asian people feel comfortable pursuing this career. Some of them may hate my work, they may think it's disgusting! And I'm sure they do - which I think is great! I think everyone should be able to love and hate - but just having the discussion about art is pretty cool, because often we don't get to do that in our communities as freely as we want to.

<u>Just finally - as someone who works with colour every day, do you have any advice for how non-artists can bring colour into their lives?</u>

The most important thing is not to be afraid of colour. Colour can create a sense of confidence and energy. Use colour intentionally. If you associate colour to an energy or a mood, and it creates a sense of peace or power, harness it! I'm also an art therapist, and I use colour with my clients therapeutically, and sometimes we find colour is terrifying, and so we create a story around it, a sense of how we can incorporate colour to work for us. Just try it out, because you might find that it brings you something, it might interrupt something that feels monotonous, or it might create a sense of balance when things feel chaotic. When I feel like absolute shit, I'll just put on red lipstick, or I'll wear something outrageously bright and I'm like 'well, it's doing the work for me', so I can just be present and move through the world.

(Centre left)

Kirthana attending to details of an early work-in-progress.

(Centre right)

The Red Sarong, 2023, oil on canvas.

Project: Casa Desa
Design: Jun Ong
Size: 83 sqm / 900 sqft
Location: Kuala Lumpur, Malaysia

INTERVIEW ELOÏSE LACHICORÉE
IMAGES JD CHANG

Setting out to seamlessly integrate storage, display space and a playground for pets into a compact home is no challenge for the faint-hearted. But Malaysian lighting artist Jun Ong was determined when it came to Casa Desa. Taking matters into his own hands, Jun designed and constructed a collection of clever storage and joinery units that would not only house and display his books, artworks and keepsakes, but would also house and entertain his two cats. The contentment of his feline companions carried as much weight in driving design decisions as Jun's desire to craft an open and welcoming home ideal for a passionate home cook, entertainer and collector. The outcome in this apartment in Kuala Lumpur is as playful as it is practical and, in largely focusing the renovation on joinery elements he could design and construct himself, Jun was able to realise his new home in only a matter of months.

What attracted you to this apartment and what was it like when you first moved in?

The unit is on the top floor of a three-storey block of flats. I was immediately drawn to the split-level nature of the building being on a slope, allowing for an interesting staircase connection overlooking a courtyard. Taman Desa (meaning 'Village Garden' in Malay) is a quiet neighbourhood found on a small hill close to downtown Kuala Lumpur and its neighbouring city, Petaling Jaya. I grew up in an area nearby so I always quite liked the idea of living in Taman Desa. I bought the apartment from a good friend who left the space in good condition with minimal built-ins.

What did you keep and what did you change?

The existing broken white marble flooring – quite a popular finish in the 1980s – was the first thing I chose to preserve, as I really liked it. The previous tenant also removed the balcony for a bigger living room space, but I decided to reinstate it, installing tall folding windows to create an indoor-outdoor living space.

What do you like to do at home and how does the design of your home make it all possible?

I love cooking, hosting and experimenting with food, hence the kitchen is the core space in my home. The open-plan nature allows the living and dining space to revolve around the kitchen too.

```
(Below)
The previous owner removed the balcony in
favour of a larger living space but Jun
reinstated it and  installed "tall folding
windows... to create an indoor-outdoor
living space."
```

Where did your inspiration for all the multifunctional built-in units come from?

My two very active cats Jasper and Juno were the inspiration behind wanting the built-ins to be both interactive and functional storage and display space.

> The idea behind the cat ramps came from being unsure of what to do with an old pillar and beam around the dining area, which I eventually decided to use as a 'cat shrine'.

The ledges suspended above the ramps act as both a resting place and sort-of-viewing-deck for the cats, as well as a place to store and display my books and art.

More recently, I designed and built a wall-mounted shelving unit consisting of six modules stacked on top of each other with interconnecting holes for the cats to climb through. Other features of the unit include a bookshelf, cable organiser, a stand mirror and more cat ramps. The offset sliding mirror doors also provide an interesting distortion of the reflected surroundings while the staggered placements of each of the shelf modules allows for interesting nooks in which to display my art collections. The inspiration behind building this additional shelving unit was the need for more space-saving storage with additional features for the cats to play with and enjoy.

```
(Right)
The design
simultaneously
caters to the
pleasures and
interests of Jun
and his cats.
```

SMALL HOMES CASA DESA

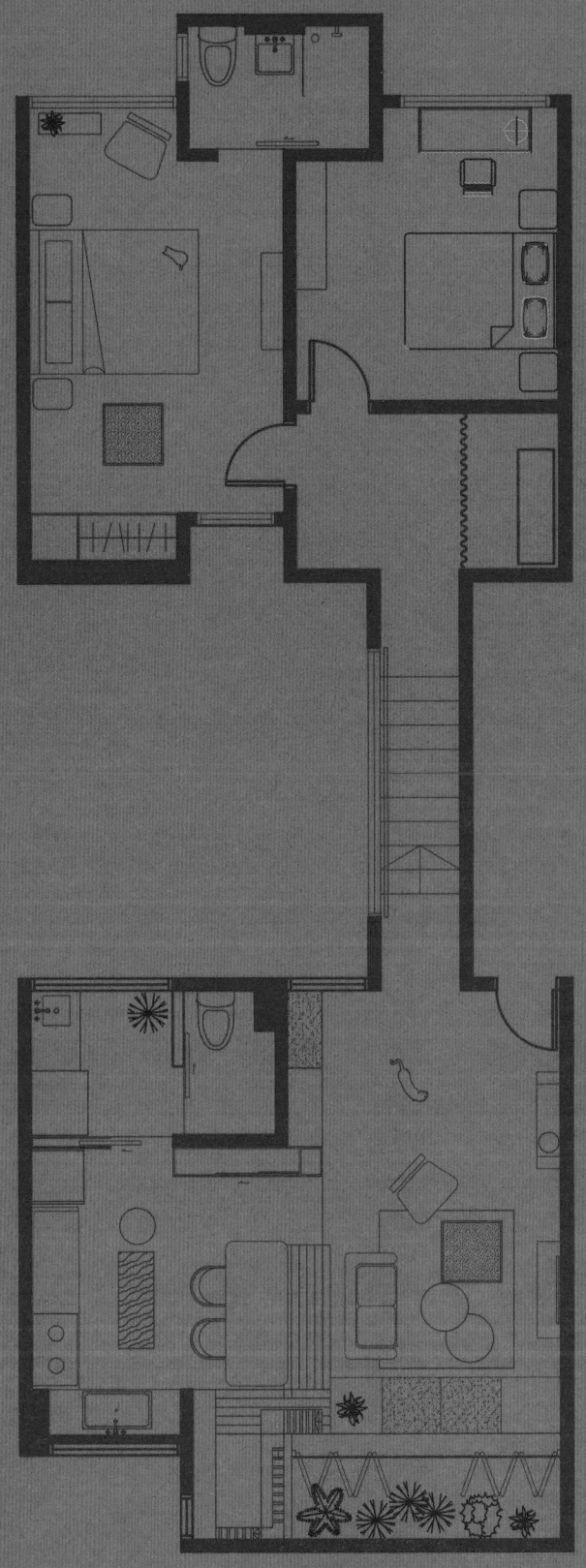

Could you talk us through the timeline of the design and build?

I bought the apartment in 2017, moved in for a year whilst planning the design, and started the renovation process in 2019. The design process was pretty quick, lasting around one month, whereas the actual renovation and building work took about three months.

Were there any surprises or unexpected challenges once you got started?

As the property is quite old there was a lot of wiring and piping that had to be hacked and replaced, which was a lengthy process but definitely necessary. Also as someone who cooks and entertains quite often I wanted to create an open-plan kitchen, dining and living space which required knocking down the wall separating the original kitchen and living room. This turned out to be quite tricky because there was an unexpected structural pillar and beam that I had to keep and which I decided to leave exposed. Although it was a bit of a challenge in deciding what to do with the pillar and beam, they served as the basis for the cat ramps and inspiration for the raw and exposed look and material palette.

What else guided your choice of materials and finishes?

I wanted the space to feel warm yet understated – playing around with pairing cheaper and more luxury materials like plywood and natural stones helped me to achieve this. Choosing to work with plywood and clear varnish as the main cabinetry material also allowed me to seamlessly integrate the cat components into the built-in cabinets. I created large circular openings on some of the cabinet doors to function as cubby holes for the cats, and swapped the cabinet door knobs to circular opening handles to match.

How did your background as a light artist influence the design?

Lighting at home is crucial for me. Ironically, being a light artist and working with advanced lighting technologies, I much prefer ambient and simple lighting at home. Though I do have ceiling downlights, I'll only use indirect lighting such as wall lights and table lamps around the apartment at night. I also pay close attention to the finishes and materials of the objects and furniture around my lighting; I really like to see how light bounces off them. I'm also big on the sensorial deprivation concept, whereby the absence of a certain sense heightens others. In this case, the lack of light at night allows my other senses to peak, and at the same time release. The lighting above my cat ramps is blue as research has shown that deep blue light calms pets. It doesn't always seem to work with them though!

Tell us more about the cats.

I've had Jasper for almost five years, since he was a kitten. I recently adopted Juno who's one year old. Jasper is a black and white tuxedo cat, whilst Juno is a black Persian cat. Seeing as I've had Jasper for longer, he and a previous cat both served as inspiration for the design of the apartment. Now Jasper plays the cool older brother showing Juno the ropes. He actually taught Juno how to climb the ramps when he was a kitten. Juno is the hyperactive one but is also clingy and loves my bed.

Speaking for yourself, Jasper and Juno, what are your favourite details in your home?

> The ramps and the balcony ledge are definitely a shared favourite. Now that there are two cats, they often play 'zoomies' down the main staircase straight up to the ramps and up to the ceiling ledge.

The balcony ledge also acts as an interesting threshold for me to connect with the outside world from inside my apartment with its tall folding windows. The height from the ledge also allows the cats to peer down to the surrounding apartment compound. Jasper and Juno also like the new shelving unit as they can both watch each other from across the living room, with one sitting on top of the shelves and the other on top of the ramp, and they also have new holes and ramps to enjoy.

(Left page)
Jasper and Juno relaxing amongst their network of ramps and hidey-holes.

While your home caters so generously to the needs and happiness of your cats, it's also filled with an eclectic mix of books, art and colourful furniture and objects. What's the key for you to make it all work?

I intentionally kept the plywood built-ins muted and raw as I wanted to use them to display my vintage furniture and objects that I love to collect. Some of my collection includes: a vintage IKEA Bogan table (1986) by Tord Bjorklund, the Etch Lamp by Tom Dixon (where I used to work in London), the iconic Artemide Tizio desk lamp by Richard Sapper and vintage brass switches from Chatuchak market in Bangkok. I also have some of my own art creations around the place such as 'Orb', an iridescent spherical module which reflects incredible lighting during the day, a custom iridescent-chromed steel plate coffee table and a custom pair of pendants above my dining table in the same material. I love collecting objects and feature pieces from my travels as they usually add pops of colour or have an interesting texture, form or funny story behind them. The same goes for the artwork, with my two favourite ones being a 3D wood-cut diorama by Malaysian artist Tomi Heri depicting a robbery scene in a back alley, and a landscape painting I have by my sister's mother-in-law, the Australian artist, Jill Bond. Beyond that, my book collection is quite varied and includes a range of art, architecture and cookbooks.

Any thoughts on how furniture and design in our homes might evolve to better suit our pets?

Two words: MICRO-FIBRE! All finishes and upholstery need to be microfibre or another sort of cut pile fabric so that your cats aren't interested in scratching them. I definitely learnt that the hard and expensive way. I think there's definitely a gap in the market for beautifully designed pet furniture – at least in Asia – that can integrate seamlessly within the home. It's actually always been a dream of mine to design some cool pet furniture. Most of my pet furniture is modular and adaptable, meaning I can scale them up or down and move them around to suit different living needs in a small unit, whilst also offering exciting play components for my pets.

```
(Top left)
The open-plan design is well-suited to Jun's
love of cooking and entertaining.

(Top right)
Jun customised "a crystal-inspired wall
lamp made from found materials, like broken
CDs and charcoal..." to be a focal point
for his bathroom.
```

We've talked a lot about your kitchen and living area but what about your bedroom and bathroom? How did you alter these spaces during the renovation?

I'm tall, so the main feature of my bedroom is my custom king-size bed with its custom micro-fibre upholstery frame which is ideal as the cats also sleep in my bedroom. I have a beautiful black and white triptych in my room too, painted by one of my favourite Malaysian abstract artists Mark Tan. The etched-paintings are flanked by two super-warm wall lamps by the Sabine Marcelis x Ikea collection.

Out of all the spaces in my apartment, the bathroom is probably where I spend most of my time unwinding. I wanted the toilet to look monochromatic and sleek, so I chose a skinny, rectangular, textured grey tile for the wall against a matching grey tiled floor. I also opted for a small mounted sink with a tall vanity mirror to add to the look. I also customised a crystal-inspired wall lamp made from found materials, like broken CDs and charcoal, which I think acts as a focal point and anchors the bathroom space nicely.

How would you describe your home in three words?

Understated, cheeky and sleek.

**Need storage?
Just add Mustard.**

mustardmade.com

Sunkissed Sheets

The very particular pleasure of sun-dried sheets.

WORDS BEC VRANA DICKINSON

I'm watching my neighbour. Not in a creepy way. Maybe I shouldn't have inserted the word creepy into this, because it's anything but. I have jazz playing after all. What I'm admiring is their swinging sun-drying sheets. Precisely hung and pegged at meticulous intervals – their canary yellow linen has been left to leisurely sway in the breeze. It's so considered, yet free, like Stan Getz's saxophone. Immediately I play out the rest of their day in my mind…

Once dried to a gentle crunch, their neat folding (if their pegging is anything to go by) will imprint a clean crisp grid onto the sheets. The linen will then sigh gusts of cleansed air as they shake the duvet into the cover and again when they lay it softly to rest on top of their flat sheet. (There's definitely a flat sheet). In the evening, there are more sighs – this time of contentment – as they pull back the duvet and recline into plumped pillows. They read to extend the ecstasy: something by Amor Towles, or Tucci if they're more non-fiction. The UV-purification means their bed smells of almost nothing, a good 'nothing', apart from a whiff of eco-friendly detergent. They've left their phones on a living room charger, so they effortlessly drift into sleep. Deep, restful sleep. When we meet accidentally sometime later I know we'll gush over something like vine-ripened tomatoes or how pine cones make the best kindling.

Standing on my balcony (the watch tower), I swivel to survey my own unfastened sheets. Draped haphazardly over the metal railing, they flap and constantly threaten to take flight with each puff of wind. I reassure my fitted sheet by readjusting it for the fifth time. I'm still considering pegs, but I've made it four years without them and will probably only succumb when I lose my sky-blue duvet cover to my other downstairs neighbour's yard. The same one that caught my orange underwear a few weeks ago. Those are still down there – I check in on them each morning while clutching a mug of instant. It's much the same today, just a little busier. It's Sunday. It's sunny. It's Sunny Sheet-Washing Sunday.

Waking to bright blue skies this morning, the urge to pull at my bed's four corners to disrupt the shared laundry with a 7am cycle was immediate. Previously forced to drape damp sheets over a ground-floor-flat's lightless hallway, I now run at each clear Sunday with peg-less vigour. My sister, who lives elsewhere, is the same, except she uses pegs and judges me because I don't. She's even more particular than my Tucci neighbours. Her pillowcases are not hung half over the line, but instead pegged from their short edge, so they dry neat and flat as if ironed. Her upstairs neighbour on the other hand leaves theirs to bunch and desiccate on the line, pegless like me, but even wilder (their clothesline is rooted in a threatening base of grassless soil). We sometimes watch them fearfully from my sister's ground-floor living room as the sheets brave the rain and continue to fly defiantly out there into the week's end.

I preach like Sunday is the only day I wash sheets, but I'm really referring to any Sun-Day. Neighbours for entertainment is an optional bonus, however, jazz is not. I like to think Nat King Cole is as good at removing bad bacteria as the sun is, but I don't want to spread rumours. It's just something I dreamed up while hanging sheets last Sun-Day.

A SHARED STILLNESS

INTERVIEW ELIZABETH PRICE
IMAGES JONAS BJERRE-POULSEN

"Across the seas, two distant regions have developed similar approaches to design and architecture that share a respect for nature, a sensitivity to light, and a dedication to craft." – Stillness

On July 8th in 1853, American naval officer Matthew C Perry led a fleet of four ships into Tokyo Bay with the intent of bullying Japan into reopening its trading ports (which had been largely closed to trade and visitors for some 200 years). The mission was a success and the effect was swift. Japonisme was the term the French coined to describe the fascination and desire that erupted for all things Japanese and the art and design movement that followed. It was not a one-way street, however – Western ideals, fashion, art and design entered Japanese culture too – and, long, long before the term Japandi entered our vernacular and Instagram feeds, recognition of a shared aesthetic and mutual admiration emerged, and a cultural exchange ensued.

The multidisciplinary practice of Copenhagen-based Norm Architects has been heavily influenced and shaped by these decades of cultural exchange as well as its own creative collaborations with Japanese designers. It is this influence and an exploration of Japanese aesthetics through a Scandinavian lens that forms the subject of a new book from Norm Architects and Gestalten – Stillness. Jonas Bjerre-Poulsen, co-founder of Norm Architects tells us how and when the love affair began for him and why the fascination endures.

Where and how did your love affair with Japanese design begin?

During my studies at the Royal Danish Academy of Fine Arts in Copenhagen, I worked as an assistant to a Danish designer who was very interested in Japan and Japanese kitchen utensils in particular. He travelled frequently to Japan and he always brought back gifts – traditional Japanese knives, bamboo baskets, ceramics, dyed fabrics and much more. It was through the delicate shapes, intricate details and master craftmanship of objects, that I first fell in love. Subsequently I started studying Japanese architecture in architecture school and wrote a paper in search of a spatial vocabulary for Japanese architecture. For many years after finishing my studies, I applied principles learned from Japan into our projects, without having ever set foot in the country.

How would you describe the shared aesthetic between Scandinavian and Japanese design?

The profound beauty of stillness we see in Japanese aesthetics is at once familiar and foreign. On one hand it feels like home and resonates with the melancholic simplicity of our Scandinavian culture – the still atmosphere of a Japanese garden or tearoom is not far from the stillness you can experience looking at the empty spaces painted by Danish artist Vilhelm Hammershøi. On the other hand, the rich cultural tapestry of Japanese architecture, crafts and gardens embodies a profound harmony between the self and the surroundings that is not found in Scandinavian design. The essence of stillness in Japanese aesthetics seems to transcend the spatial to create space to breathe, and space to immerse oneself in a state of mind that awakens the innate longing for a connection with our primordial home: nature. It is within this interval that the essence of stillness resides.

Through the poetic interplay of light and shadow, form and emptiness, Japanese architecture and design evoke a profound sense of tranquility, inviting us to dwell in the present moment with mindfulness and grace.

(Page 108)

This is Maana Homes: a pair of guest houses designed by Kyoto-based architect Shigenori Uoya - an expert in restoring traditional machiya houses. The designs blend historical and contemporary Japanese design elements.

(Right)

One of the suites in Maana Homes' Maana Kiyomizu in Kyoto.

(Below)

The careful arrangement of objects in relation to *Ma* (a Japanese concept of 'pause' or 'negative space') is thought to create a sense of calmness and tranquility.

(Right)

Traditional Japanese buildings often feature walls made of earth, straw or other natural materials, known as 'tsuchikabe'.

(Page 112)

Heatherhill Beach House by Norm Architects, Vejby Strand, Denmark.

(Page 113)

The main tatami mat room in the traditional wooden house belonging to Japanese tea ceremony master Dairik Amae on the forested hilltop of the Daitoku-ji temples in northern Tokyo.

Images:
Jonas Bjerre-Poulsen,
Stillness, gestalten 2024.

Exploring Japanese aesthetics from a Scandinavian perspective has been a journey of curiosity as as well as introspection. In our attempt to unveil defining elements and ideas in Japanese architecture and design, we have also sought to understand the kinship between our Scandinavian heritage and that of Japan – and how one culture has influenced the other – as well as to ponder the timeless allure of Japanese aesthetics.

Architecture and design have always been shaped by culture, history, and the environment in which they are created. Architects and designers often look to other cultures for inspiration, incorporating elements into their own work to create buildings and furniture that, in an evolutionary process, become new, cross-cultural hybrids. Cultural exchange opens our minds, fosters respect and has the power to elevate the nations that engage in such exchange. Danish architecture and design has in the 20th century been greatly inspired by Japanese aesthetics in their use of natural materials, open space plans, wood joinery, simplicity and essentialism.

<u>Where, would you say, the lines blur between Scandinavian and Japanese aesthetics and where do they diverge?</u>

For centuries, Japan has captivated hearts worldwide with its artful mastery of simplicity, asymmetry and naturalism. From serene gardens, temples and shrines, to the intricate details of high-quality craftsmanship, Japanese aesthetics have left a pleasing and emotionally resonant mark on global design culture. Through numerous meaningful and memorable visits to Japan, with camera in hand, at Norm Architects we have carefully studied and documented the spaces and places we have experienced to better understand them, and we have attempted to learn how the Japanese have created such enchanting atmospheres of stillness. From the shores of Scandinavia where we reside, our fascination with Japanese aesthetics has prompted a deeper exploration – a journey to uncover the parallels between two seemingly disparate realms, one built on the foundation of a strict Protestant peasant society, and the other on Shintoist and Buddhist philosophies.

We have observed that Scandinavian and Japanese aesthetics share minimalist approaches characterised by clean lines, unadorned forms and uncluttered spaces. Both styles prioritise simplicity and functionality, with an emphasis on creating spaces that are beautiful, sensory and practical.

In both countries, there is a strong emphasis on using natural materials. I also think that both places, due to their climate and changing seasons, have a strong connection with the outdoors, often blurring the boundaries between interior and exterior – maybe more so in Japan. However, I think that the most evident similarity might be found in a love for simple unadorned craftsmanship, using quality materials with an attention to detail.

Traditional Scandinavian design often features light woods such as oak, birch, beech and pine, as well as natural materials such as leather and wool, that is not as commonly used in Japan. In contrast, Japanese design frequently incorporates darker patinated or burned woods such as cedar and cypress, as well as paper, bamboo, and stone, that we do not find in Denmark. I guess it reflects the geographical location and the natural resources we have been able to refine. Scandinavian design in general also tends to favour a light, neutral colour palette, with whites, greys, and light wood tones predominating. In Japanese design, on the other hand, there is a wider range of muted earthy colors, such as greens, browns, and indigos, that we have been inspired by.

What has been the greatest influence of Japanese design on you as a designer?

Everything I have described in the book and much more. It is impossible to single something out.

***

Stillness: An Exploration of Japanese Aesthetics in Architecture and Design co-edited by Norm Architects and Gestalten is published by Gestalten. Visit gestalten.com | normcph.com

A SOFT SIDE

INTERVIEW BEC VRANA DICKINSON

It all started with a jug for designer Layla Cluer. A deceptively large porcelain jug. Generous enough to fill the glasses of 20 guests, playful enough to complement the party and still light enough to get the job done. A jug for big gatherings and not leaving the table. This jug soon led to the birth of Softedge Studio. Informed by a background in architecture, fine art and curatorial practice, Softedge Studio has become a vehicle for Layla's curious and creative experimentation with domestic objects.

Designed on Bundjalung country/Byron Bay, the studio's porcelain tableware is now made in Hasami, a small Japanese town with more than 400 years of porcelain production expertise. Carefully handcrafted, Softedge Studio's collection of tableware looks how you imagine the perfect porridge spoon would feel. Inexplicably smooth and comforting. Something you decide you need, not want. Like the 'Everything Bowl' – perfect for... well, everything.

How has your background in architecture, fine art and curation shaped your approach to designing ceramics?

It's made for a really rich set of references. I like being creatively ambidextrous and pushing myself in different directions. Studying architecture at age 17 left its mark on me. Quite early on I was lucky enough to become a research assistant, which allowed me to engage with architecture through a theoretical lens and this eventually led me to study fine art. My interest in architecture was diverse but it was architects, who used drawing and other artistic mediums to explore their ideas conceptually that interested me most. Diller + Scofidio's early installation work *Indigestion* and Sarah Wigglesworth's diagrammatic drawing series (that studied how a formal dinner party setting changes throughout a meal) were a few of the many works I came across that straddled this line. I love the use of narrative and drawing to explore our relationships with each other, objects and spaces. This really informed how I think of making objects – fun pieces, with a function.

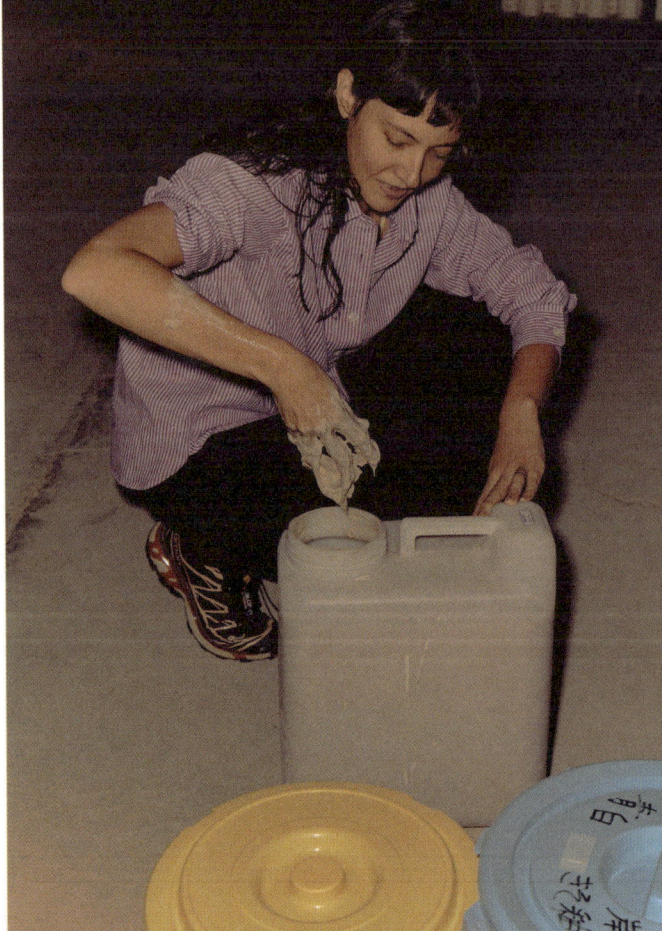

From the ideation and design, through to the making and glazing process, all of Softedge's porcelain pottery pieces are approached with playfulness whilst keeping functionality at their core. Images: Annika Kafcaloudis, courtesy of Softedge Studio.

Your 'rolled rim' range creates such a calm sense of movement. What inspired it?

The initial idea came from the medieval myth of *Cockaigne*: a land of plenty, where rivers run with wine, cheese grows on trees, and roads are paved with pastry. It was the early pandemic days when there were shortages and we couldn't get together.

> I was craving that sense of indulgence around people, that collective experience when you eat so much you have to pop your pants open and your rolls spill over – that feeling of abundance.

I played around with distilling that idea into an object, a small sculptural gesture. The end product also enhances functionality, as the exaggerated rims make the products harder to break, extending their lifespan.

All of your production is carried out in Hasami, Japan. How did this collaboration begin?

The main drive to manufacture overseas was quality, plus growth in demand, material shortages and a shifting team. Producing everything in Byron Bay became quite challenging, so in 2023, I wound down the studio. Later, while visiting Japan, I was passing through Hasami on my way to Arita (the birthplace of Japanese porcelain) and I started chatting with the owner of a cafe. I showed him my work, and then a few phone calls later, I was being shown around Hasami and learning how the town's small family-run workshops collaborate to handcraft their local ceramics. Hasami was it, I actually danced down the street that night.

How do your pieces come to life from the initial design to the final product?

It's an iterative design process. There's a lot of back-and-forth between the digital and physical. I worked with a friend from architecture school, who's great at parametrics, to digitise the original rolled rim pieces. We even wrote a script to help manipulate the rims and bowl profiles so they could neatly stack. Once we were happy with the digital model, we printed out a 3D model for the master mould maker. There were many months of tweaks, testing the way each glaze interacted with the shape in the kiln. With hundreds of years of expertise, Hasami is the perfect place for all this, we even have an 14th-generation glaze expert on the team. We collaborate with a local trading company, Maruhiro Inc., to manage the production process. Ryusei Tasaki, also known as Softedge Sensei, is in charge there.

What would be your dream meal to eat off your gorgeous plates and bowls?

I'd have Ruth Rogers from the River Cafe in London cook for me, for a start. I love her story and that she's not a trained chef. Everything she conceives is so beautiful yet simple, it's always about quality. It would be a big 'family meal' spread, like the ones I cook for the Maruhiro team at the end of my trips to Japan. Each time I try to cook them a different cuisine, usually something Mediterranean, and always with plenty of olive oil.

(Left)
"The exaggerated rims make the products harder to break, extending their lifespan."
Image: Annika Kafcaloudis, courtesy of Softedge Studio.

(Right)
"We even wrote a script to help manipulate the rims and bowl profiles so they could neatly stack." Image: courtesy of Softedge Studio.

A Matter of Context

WORDS ELIZABETH PRICE
IMAGES NAM TRAN

The art of interior styling can feel like indecipherable witchcraft to many of us. (How is it that some people just *know* what goes with what?) Ben Mooney, a Melbourne based curator, collector, stylist is someone who has found his calling in this field. We visit Ben's beautiful home and store to experience how he uses the power of context to help others unlock the mysterious codes of what goes with what.

Ben Mooney in his charming and beautifully curated store, Ma House Supply Store in Melbourne's Collingwood.

I'm surprised to learn that Ben Mooney hasn't been doing this for long. Well, not professionally at least. The collecting part started when he was just five years old. It was a Murano glass paperweight at a garage sale that captured the eye of that precocious little boy. There was just something about the way it seemed to *hold* light and the pleasing weight of the object in his tiny hand. Treasure.

"I think shiny things are a thing to me. I mean, I don't think I'm into glitz and glam, but I do really like things that play with light or have a shine or a sparkle to them," Ben tells me.

Ben's current home and the base for his business is no exception. The way light enters the building at different times of day, changing the character of the spaces and playing with the shiny things within them was a key attraction. It was the discovery of this two-storey corner building in Melbourne's Collingwood that became one of those sliding doors moments for Ben.

(Below)
Ben and Goody in his courtyard garden.

"It was really beautiful. I dolled it up and started renting it out for shoots and a lot of people just wanted to buy my stuff all the time. So I thought, 'Let's just start a shop'."

The shop, Ma House Supply Store is on the ground level of the space and upstairs is where Ben and Goody – his handsome Italian greyhound – live. With both spaces available and in high demand for film shoots, photo shoots and events, the pair are kept very busy.

It seems people can't get enough of Ben's aesthetic and curatorial eye. It's so particular. And so pleasing. Objects imbued with whimsy and quirk sit alongside austere antiques, serious ceramics and crystal, contemporary design pieces and flea market finds. As someone lacking Ben's obvious talents, it's hard for me to understand or decipher how all of it *works*. Because it does. Without question. The spaces Ben curates and styles are spaces in which you want to linger and as you do, they continue to unfurl and reward you with further discoveries of delightful details. There are some patterns that begin to emerge too. In addition to being drawn to glass objects, Ben has "a thing for faces" and metal objects too.

"I think a lot of shoppers need context to see things in a different light," Ben says.

(Top left)

Ben's 'face vase' upstairs in his home is something that people "try to buy off [him] all the time" but sadly it is not for sale.

(Top right)

The inexpensive metal bowl that has prompted Ben to consider launching his own line of vases and other decorative pieces.

Long before I visited Ben, I fell in love with a metal bowl that I had seen in previously published photos of his space. Its abstracted hand-like shape is at once sculptural and simple and it has appeared regularly in photos of Ben's space over the years. Ben thinks it's an early 2000s relic from a high street store. So, nothing fancy. But boy, does it look fancy next to a black terracotta 'Tang' horse sculpture atop a vintage timber bureau with intricate inlay detailing. It's a favourite of Ben's too and incidentally, a piece that prompted him to ponder launching his own line of decorative metal objects. Watch this space. I'm curious to know: where does this natural talent of Ben's stem from? How did five-year-old Ben know a lump of Murano glass when he saw it?

"I think my mum had great taste but I didn't grow up with my mum – I grew up with my dad. He had worked in antiques for a little while and somehow we still had some when I was a kid, but then we lost them," Ben remembers. "We really didn't have much money and I grew up in the country. I really didn't think that there was much beauty where I was."

"So when you're constantly trying to zoom in on beauty and there's not much around, I think it does something to you. And so when you are at an age where you can afford to buy things yourself, you go crazy."

These days Ben's beautiful wares are mainly sourced from vintage markets. Ideally, places crammed to the rafters with furniture, decorative objects, artworks and curiosities. "I love it when there's a lot to choose from. A lot of people get overwhelmed by those places, but that's my happy place," Ben says. "And one thing that helps me in my business is that everyone who works in antiques or vintage is fucking weird. And I'm weird as well. So we all get along." Ben's advice for amateurs is to always look up. "I mean, it's sort of like aisles at the supermarket, if you're looking for the Weetbix, they might be on the bottom shelf – so you start at the top and scan all the way along and down."

Ben gets a kick when people think he sources his pieces internationally. While his personal collection of treasures upstairs includes mementos from his pre-pandemic travels ("I really do have a terrible memory and objects can really spark that memory for me."), everything in the store is sourced locally.

Ben has been a collector "forever". When he sees a beautiful thing that speaks to him with its form, materiality, charm or craftsmanship it's difficult to walk away but the store has assumed a crucial role in servicing his acquisitory desires without risking over expansion of his own collection upstairs.

The living area of Ben's home above Ma House Supply Store – a space he regularly rents out for photo shoots, film shoots and events.

Ben confesses to having "a lot of coffee pots", a slight addiction to anything featuring a Willow pattern and loving "kitchen things that kind of look evil."

"I have a bit of a shopping addiction, so it helps with that," Ben says. I proffer that there must be times, though, when Ben feels conflicted: how does he decide what is for the store and what is for Ben? "It's very hard," he admits. "But I don't take things upstairs. That's the rule."

It's a solid rule. Because once Ben sees a new object in context, in his home, immediately befriending all his other things and somehow assuming this sudden familiarity and sense of belonging, it's hard to let go. And this here is Ben's particular talent and the magic of Ma House Supply Store – it's all about the context. To you or me, a bronze bowl, crystal vase or scuffed statue in the jumbled atmosphere of an antiques store jammed in alongside tea services and tapestried furniture, might read as naff (or might escape our eye entirely). But, once liberated and thoughtfully placed beside other objects (that you never could have imagined would belong together), its full potential emerges.

"It's like when you go to these places and there's shit everywhere and you can't imagine anything in your own home. Bring it somewhere else though and it sort of unlocks itself," Ben says. "I feel like I'm rescuing all these things and bringing them to the right owners. I think a lot of shoppers need context to see things in a different light."

"A lot of customers that started with me when I opened, I've watched their taste develop and it's not necessarily like a copy of mine. It's just that they're seeing things in a different way than they did before."

Ben has a front row seat to this flourishing confidence too as many of his customers become his friends. "I really, I didn't expect this to happen. You always think when you start a business that it'll just be your friends who are your customers, but your friends are not your customers. Your customers are people that you never knew, but a lot of my regulars are definitely friends," Ben reflects.

"If they're buying things from other places, they'll say, 'I've got this great rug.' And I'm like, 'Well done. I'm proud of you. That's a beautiful rug'."

And it's not all vintage in Ma House Supply Store either. Ben supports a select stable of local contemporary designers, artists and artisans by stocking their pieces and products in his store – Sean Brickhill, Hattie Malloy and Christopher Myles, to name a few. Supporting other creatives is a passion for Ben but the combination of new and old also just makes the space more interesting, he says. "I think their style is very refined and contemporary and that for me is a perfect mix for the store and helps uplift everything else."

It does feel like a perfect mix and this harmony between new and old guided by Ben's keen curatorial eye resonates throughout each room within his home and the store alike. For people like me who lack the patience, tenacity and guiding instincts to successfully scour vintage marketplaces for hidden gems, he's done the hard work for us. It's all on a platter, or at least in a context that invites us to imagine and covet.

Details from Ben's home including a framed photograph that his father left him when he died. This photograph of David Bowie was taken by a close friend of Ben's father during Bowie's time in Australia while filming his music videos for *Let's Dance* and *China Girl* in the early 80s.

BEN'S TIPS FOR STYLING YOUR HOME

Styling should be a response to place.

"Think about your base coat – being the room itself. This means considering its characteristics and dimensions and the colours and light you have to work with. In other places I've lived, it's always a response to that place. It's not necessarily like, 'oh, this place is going to have these busts everywhere and these big lights or whatever'. If I lived in a really tiny place, I would not have the same set up. But here I'm working with the dimensions of the room and going, I know it can carry it. And you sort of have to live up to the room in a way. From there, start with your biggest things first, whether that's your couch or dining table."

Favour what you love over styles and trends.

"Whoever said the things that you love will kind of magically go together was right. I think that it's very true. I mean, all the colours that I love in a way are kind of a family anyway. I think you really have to buy what you love and not just, you know, 'paint a style'."

Make it inviting.

Ben strives for the spaces in his home to appear very comfortable – spaces that beckon you to sit and spend time in them. The rooms in Ben's home and store feature clusters or curations of objects that invite closer inspection and reward curiosity.

Make room for happy accidents.

While we all strive for a sense of our homes being 'done' or 'complete', Ben says you've also got to make room for accidents. "A good thing about having the shop and having to style the shop is you're always moving things around and you might have to move everything off that table to clean it. Then you have these happy accidents: 'oh, my God. That vase looks beautiful next to that!'"

Tune into your emotions.

"With every object or every scene that I set up there is something emotional about it for me. While it might never feel complete, there has to be that feeling of 'this is nice'."

Containment works against clutter.

While Ben has an enormous collection, and shelves in the kitchen and living area are jam packed with beautiful things, they are lightly organised into collections that make sense together. But mostly importantly, Ben notes, "It's contained. I think that is the trick. You can't let it spill over everywhere. I always try to keep surfaces like coffee tables and my dining table relatively clear." Ben says he's still a collector at the end of the day and if you are too, "You have to find the best way to display your wares."

Reasons to venture into vintage…

"With so much cheap stuff out there I just think people are silly not to. It's usually high quality as it's already lasted this long. But you have to like things. I don't want anyone to buy something that they don't like. So if you don't like vintage, that's fine. You don't have to like vintage. You do you. I love all periods and all styles, but that's me."

WHAT
WE DO WITH THE
SHADOWS

WORDS JAMES SHACKELL

He was born in Guadalajara and ended up as a literal diamond. In between, he changed Latin architecture forever. Meet Luis Barragán, the grandfather of Mexican Modernism.

In September 2015, an American conceptual artist named Jill Magid, along with two grave-diggers and a bunch of official notaries, entered the Rotonda de los Jaliscienses Ilustres in Guadalajara to dig up the ashes of Mexican architect Luis Barragán. It had been 27 years since the great man had passed away from Parkinson's complications, and his copper urn was (by now) heavily oxidized.

Opening the lid, Magid carefully scooped up half a kilogram of ash – all that remained of one of the 20th century's greatest creative geniuses – and transferred the grey powder into a plastic bag. The next day, she flew back to New York with Luis Barragán in her carry-on luggage.

This is the story of a self-taught architect from Guadalajara who somehow became the grandfather of Latin American Modernism. A man whose not-so-humble, two-bedroom home was considered so culturally significant that UNESCO declared it a World Heritage Site in 2004. His full name was Luis Ramiro Barragán Morfín, but he tended to go by 'Luis Barragán', or even just Barragán. (Like Mozart or Picasso, once you reach a sufficient cultural altitude, one name is enough.)

Born to a wealthy Catholic family in 1902, Barragán is arguably Latin America's most influential architect. He was the first Mexican to win the field's highest honour, the Pritzker Prize, and since his death in 1988 his work and general vibe has taken on a kind of fabled status; so much so that some critics think he's in danger of becoming a caricature.

(Page 132)
Known for being one of Barragán's most iconic projects, La Cuadra San Cristóbal features an equestrian compound, along with arches and beams in Barragán's signature shade of pink. Image: Adam Wiseman/iStock.

(Left)
Barragán's Cuadra San Cristóbal, Los Clubes (1966-68), Mexico City, Mexico. With horses featuring in many of Barragán's earliest childhood memories, his love of horses was reflected in many of his architectural designs. Image: © Rene Burri/Magnum Photos (1969).

"More and more, Barragán is becoming the Frida Kahlo of architecture," Frederica Zanco, head of the controversial Barragan Foundation, once told a journalist. "People ask for pictures… then you see them in a spread in a fashion magazine for something about how pink is the new colour for spring."

In high-end architectural circles, the phrase 'Barragán-esque' gets chucked around a lot. So what does it mean? Well, Barragán mostly became known as the guy that made modernism fun.

His style was characterised by fearless colour – particularly blues, yellows, and that curious bougainvillea shade of Mexican pink – monolithic shapes, clean lines and other stuff that's harder to quantify: silence, mystery, revelation and solitude.

In Barragán's opinion, shadows were a "basic human need", and he ditched modernism's obsession with glass in favour of private spaces, hidden spaces. Secluded worlds of gentle loneliness.

"In alarming proportions the following words have disappeared from architectural publications: beauty, inspiration, magic, sorcery, enchantment, and also serenity, mystery, silence, privacy, astonishment," he said once. "All of these have found a loving home in my soul."

Architect Louis Kahn called Barragán "completely remarkable" and labelled the artist's UNESCO-listed home – which became known as Casa Luis Barragán – "not merely a house, but House itself." Nobel Prize-winning poet, Octavio Paz, described Barragán's work as "an oasis in the chaos of modernity."

In his acceptance speech for the Pritzker Prize, Barragán stated that 'Any work of architecture that does not express serenity is a mistake'. Gilardi House, a townhouse project in Mexico City, built by Barragán between 1975-1977. Image: © Luis Barragan. PROLITTERIS/Copyright Agency, 2025.

La Cuadra San Cristóbal's equestrian compound and courtyard.
Image: © Luis Barragan. PROLITTERIS/Copyright Agency, 2025.

The Reflection pool in Gálvez House, Mexico City. The brim of the basin's water is made level with the house's interior floor and reflects the calming scenes of the sky above. Image: © Luis Barragan. PROLITTERIS/Copyright Agency, 2025.

Barragán's private, reflective personality is mirrored in the quiet serenity of his personal residence Barragán House, once explaining that "My house is my refuge, an emotional piece of architecture, not a cold piece of convenience." Image: © Luis Barragan. PROLITTERIS/Copyright Agency, 2025.

"He was one of the few architects who could make modernism feel ancient, timeless, and deeply human," added historian William J.R. Curtis."

To understand Barragán the architect, you need to get to know Barragán the man. One of nine siblings, Barragán was tall, bald from a young age, and a devout Catholic. He liked to wear foppish English sports coats, ascots, silk shirts and ties. The dude even died in a tailored tweed jacket. He employed a chauffeur and a maid and hung out at equestrian centres. He was generous and warm, but also intensely private (maybe not a surprise, having grown up with eight brothers and sisters). "Art is made by the alone, for the alone," he used to say.

In fact, that's one prevailing criticism of Barragán's work: most of the houses he designed were hidden behind anonymous grey walls, or locked away in gated communities. Even Casa Luis Barragán looks cold and unwelcoming from the outside, like a modernist concrete prison.

He was a famously undemocratic architect – a friendly, inspired, big-hearted snob, but a snob nonetheless. When someone accused him of "only designing homes for rich people" he allegedly shot back, "and horses."

And yet... and yet, his work has this enduring humanism and naked emotion that keeps sucking people in. Even 70-odd years later. More than most architects, his buildings feel alive.

Keith Eggener, another historian, once told a journalist that when he visited Barragán's house in Mexico City, "I remember having this feeling of really wanting to spend the night there – not just to sleep in the house but to sleep with the house."

As a young man, Barragán studied civil engineering, and modernism might have turned out quite differently if he hadn't set sail for Europe in 1924. On his travels, he ingested as many architectural styles as humanly possible – from Bauhaus in Germany to Le Corbusier in France, Islamic frescos in Alhambra and Moorish design in North Africa. In 1925, he visited the International Exhibition of Modern Decorative and Industrial Arts in Paris and got his first taste of radical modernism.

When the young Barragán returned to Mexico in 1926, his brain was practically fizzing with potential ideas. Civil engineering suddenly seemed boring and stale compared to the world of architecture, what he referred to as "the sublime act of poetic imagination."

By the 1930s, Barragán had established himself as a competent architect, and it was around 1936 that his buildings took on a more functionalist style: see the Duplex in the Colonia Hipódromo (1936), or the Four Painters' Studios on Plaza Melchor Ocampo (1939).

But Barragán's real genius was yet to emerge. After two decades trying to blend various influences into a cohesive, original aesthetic, in the 1940s, Barragán finally cracked the code, and over the next few decades he cranked out banger after banger.

Small, one-of-a-kind homes that would re-shape the modernist movement and put Latin American architecture firmly on the map. Barragán-esque had arrived, and it was freaking glorious.

Small, one-of-a-kind homes that would re-shape the modernist movement and put Latin American architecture firmly on the map. Barragán-esque had arrived, and it was freaking glorious.

The 'Fuente de los Amantes' within Barragán's Cuadra San Cristóbal, Los Clubes (1966-68), Mexico City, Mexico. La Cuadra San Cristóbal has played backdrop to several fashion and advertising campaigns, including a Louis Vuitton ad campaign in 2016. Image: © Rene Burri/Magnum Photos (1969).

Some of these famous works included Barragán's own home, a colour-dipped sanctuary in Mexico City's working-class Tacubaya neighbourhood; the Chapel of the Capuchinas, a divinely-inspired prayer hall, swimming in yellow light; and arguably Barragán's most iconic work, the Cuadra San Cristóbal, a private-residence-and-horse-stables-turned-modernist-paradise, and a property that practically screams Vogue photoshoot. Photographer René Burri famously captured the project in 1969, and Louis Vuitton even used the space for an ad campaign in 2016.

So now we come to the thorny question. If you haven't heard of Luis Barragán before, why the heck not?

Well, it's a long story. After his death in 1988, Barragán's works, documents and sketches were entrusted to his business partner, Raul Ferrera. In 1993, Ferrera hanged himself across the street from Barragán's house, and the archive passed to Ferrera's widow, who spent years trying to sell it to various Mexican institutions. After a long and complex custody chain, the collection wound up with Federica Zanco, an Italian architectural historian, and her partner, Rolf Fehlbaum, chairman of Swiss furniture company Vitra.

> In 1994, the couple flew to New York and bought Barragán's entire archive for three million dollars, shipping everything back to a temperature-controlled, underground vault in Switzerland. The collection contained over 13,000 drawings, more than 80 photographic panels, plus endless reams of Barragán's notes, clippings, scribbles and personal correspondence.

In 1996, Zanco set up the Barragan (sic) Foundation to administer the collection, and everything seemed to be going well... until no-one was allowed access. Journalists, historians, architects and students who asked to see Barragán's archive were politely (or sometimes not-so-politely) turned away. The Foundation also tried to control Barragán's name and image licensing rights, and their prickly, litigious stance spooked galleries around the world.

And so, for over 20 years, while Zanco painstakingly catalogued all the various pieces, Barragán's body of work was – basically – lost. Buried underground behind a very heavy and well-engineered Swiss door.

Which is where American conceptual artist Jill Magid enters the story. Hearing that Rolf Fehlbaum had bought Zanco the Barragán archive as an engagement present, in lieu of a ring – a story that Zanco has since debunked – Magid got the Barragán family's permission to exhume the artist's ashes and turn them into a literal diamond[1]. And that's exactly what she did. (At the end of the day, we're really just walking-talking carbon.)

In 2016, Magid presented the compressed essence of Luis Barragán – a 2.02 carat rough-cut diamond with a single polished facet – to Zanco, basically offering her the artist's body in exchange for his body of work. Zanco was touched by the offer, but ultimately refused, deciding to hold onto the archive in Switzerland.

Thankfully, this whole weird, bureaucratic mess was resolved in May 2022, when the collection was officially, finally, opened to the public. Zanco had finished her lonely, secretive work, and Luis Barragán was released back into the world. You can visit the exhibition yourself next time you're in Weil am Rhein, Germany, just over the river from Basel.

And the diamond? As far as we know, Jill Magid still has it. The ring has been displayed in various exhibitions, including at the University Museum of Contemporary Art (MUAC) in Mexico City. And (family differences aside) it's kind of nice to think of Barragán living on, not in some airless Guadalajara tomb, but out in the light, brilliant and unyielding – a little shard of eternity. Diamonds, like architects, are forever.

---

1 Archigram, Superstudio and Gruppo Strum were like the psychedelic rock stars of 1960s architecture and design. From futuristic 'walking cities' to cities without buildings at all – these collectives helped articulate a very different, very weird design language, which paved the way for groups like Memphis.

WORDS JAMES SHACKELL

LOOK AT ALL THE

LONELY PEOPLE

PHOTOS PAUL KESSEL

There's no getting around it: we live in the Age of Loneliness. Hyper-connected, always online, surrounded by billions of people – lonely as an oyster. It's a peculiarly modern problem, and it seems to be getting worse. So what's the answer?

On 20 March, 2020, New York City went into COVID lockdown, and street photographer Paul Kessel found himself trapped inside his apartment. It could have been worse, perhaps. Paul lives high above the corner of Central Park West and West 63rd Street, with the kind of Manhattan views you usually associate with political dramas starring Brian Cox.

While other New Yorkers had to content themselves with airshafts and fire escapes, Paul could (at least) sit by his window and watch the spring clouds blow over Central Park. Still, he was a street photographer without a street, and, after a few weeks, his shutter finger began to itch…

"I was used to being on the street every day searching for photos," Paul tells me from New York. "But the pandemic drastically altered pedestrian traffic, and it felt unsafe to be outside and mingling with others, so I stayed home in my apartment."

To pass the days filled with equal parts boredom and fear, Paul started taking self-portraits, but the results were flat and uninspired. As someone who fed off noise and movement, and New York's patented *hey-I'm-walkin'-here* spontaneity, the idea of shooting himself at home, alone, quietly eating toast, didn't do much for Paul's creative juices. "It seemed meaningless to me," he laments. "I had no good ideas." But then inspiration struck out of the ether. Maybe he wasn't alone, not really.

Paul still had a mannequin in the apartment from an old studio lighting course, and he took a few test shots of its dead-eyed plastic face. Soon he was on Amazon ordering lifeless heads and cheap synthetic wigs. And while the death toll rose, and the streets went quiet, and the world closed its doors and retreated inside, Paul began eagerly shooting his new group of friends. The project would eventually form a collection, *Solitary*[1]. As in confinement.

"In the beginning, I still had no idea what the point was, of any of this," Paul says. "It then occurred to me that maybe I should shoot in the street photography style. Somehow that got me going. It could be spontaneous and not conceptualised. I started to fantasise various situations with myself and the rest of the cast. Gradually, interactions took place. In my mind I made up stories about the mannequins and me.

"In the end, there was a portfolio of photos with a narrative – and my finger no longer itched."

Deprived of human company, Paul invented his own, and looking back with five years' worth of hindsight, *Solitary* seems to neatly capture the unhinged isolation and social trauma of those early COVID lockdowns, when it felt like the world was spinning loose, unplugged from its normal programming. No-one knew what to do, or what was coming next, or even if there would be a next.

And so we get images of Paul naked in the shower, alone, surrounded by disembodied heads. Drinking wine in a dressing gown, alone, while imaginary friends sit down to lunch. Curled up in bed, alone, with a mannequin resting tenderly on his shoulder. Without genuine connection, or interaction, or the warmth of physical contact, Paul created a simulacrum of the real thing, which you can either interpret as profound or creepy (or both). *Solitary* is like the uncanny valley of human relationships.

"Anytime there is a lack of social engagement, it results in increased craziness," Paul says. "The human is a social animal."

As a photography collection, *Solitary* really resonated with people, generating a modicum of viral buzz and showing up in several magazines (including this one). But to understand why it touched a collective nerve, we have to zoom out and look at a larger societal trend: loneliness.

The truth is, despite the global population ticking over 8.2 billion, we live in a lonely world. And it's getting lonelier.

The research suggests we were lonely before COVID, and we're certainly lonely after it. According to a 2023 Meta-Gallup survey, almost

---

[1] For more of Paul's traditional, non-mannequin-related work, please turn to page 153 of your magazine.

a quarter of adults worldwide feel lonely. That's more than one billion people. The World Health Organization (WHO) has declared loneliness a global public health concern, right up there with cancer and mosquito-borne diseases, and launched an international commission to investigate the problem.

Loneliness doesn't seem to discriminate based on wealth: developing nations, industrialised nations, wealthy nations, poorer nations – loneliness can afflict anyone at any time. Just because you're not lonely today, statistically speaking, doesn't mean you won't be lonely tomorrow. There's no gender differential either: men and women seem to feel loneliness in roughly equal measure.

Paradoxically, loneliness does seem to bite hardest in cities, where it's known as "urban loneliness" – that peculiar modernist hell of being lonely together. According to some studies, the more people we have around us, and the denser those people are packed, the more lonely humans tend to feel. And considering about 56 per cent of the world's population – 4.4 billion people – live in cities, the scale of this thing is hard to overstate. People are hesitant to use the word 'pandemic' these days, for obvious reasons, but when it comes to loneliness we're definitely facing something pandemic-ish. A very real and physical threat to global health and happiness.

"The first step to fixing this is to acknowledge what loneliness is, and what it's not," says Associate Professor Michelle Lim, clinical psychologist and Scientific Chair of Australian-based not-for-profit, Ending Loneliness Together.

"Loneliness used to be seen as a personal matter, something we don't ask about. But what we realised over the last 20-odd years of scientific research is that loneliness is a normal biological signal for us to reach out to other people. It's your body's way of telling you there's an unmet need, like hunger. In this case, the need for meaningful connection."

The challenge has always been getting people (i.e. governments and policy makers) to treat urban loneliness as what it is: a public health crisis. There's been some progress on this front, but Dr Lim says the scrabble for public funding is a constant battle.

(Page 144 - 148)
Photos from Paul Kessel's *Solitary* collection all taken in his New York apartment during the pandemic lockdowns of 2020.

Whichever way you slice it, research suggests that a lack of social connection can be as harmful as 15 cigarettes a day. Lonely people are two times more likely to have chronic disease and 4.6 times more likely to experience depression. They're less productive at work, less engaged in physical activities and five times more likely to commit suicide. In a kind of dark, poetic twist, we tend to experience the physical symptoms of loneliness in exactly the place you might expect.

"There's something about loneliness and the heart," muses Dr Lim. "We have emerging studies now that show cardiovascular ageing in young people who are lonely. These are young people – we're talking about 22 year olds – who don't have a history of cardiovascular disease, but they show significantly increased signs of vascular ageing."

Of course, like many complex public health issues, while the *effects* of urban loneliness are simple and well understood, the *causes*, and more importantly what to do about them, are much fuzzier.

How can we make our cities less lonely? How can we encourage not just social interaction – people have annoying social interactions every single day – but meaningful connection? And what incentives can governments and health organisations offer to make this stuff happen? Brilliant people all over the world are working on this problem as we speak. Some of them are architects.

"Architecture alone can't solve loneliness, but it can help alleviate it by creating environments that encourage organic connection," says Maya Shpiro, Social Impact and Co-Creation Lead at international architecture firm, Henning Larsen.

It's an attractive idea. Architects (at least the best ones) have long believed that design can influence human behaviour – the so-called Architectural Determinism[2], also known as the school of Built It And They Will Come. Names like Oscar Newman, Jane Jacobs and Kevin Lynch were frontrunners in the field, and the concept has been kicking around since the middle of the 20th century, if not way earlier. Rome had the bathhouse, Renaissance Italy had the piazza, Enlightenment Europe made coffeehouses a thing. These days we call it 'human-centred design'. Making buildings to fit people, rather than the other way around.

"There's no single formula," Maya says, "but successful spaces often share principles that respond to human complexity. They accommodate a range of uses and experiences, from places to linger and people-watch to areas for movement or quiet solitude. Uniform, standardised environments can feel alienating because they don't reflect the messiness or spontaneity of real life."

Maya begins rattling off examples. There's Sydney's Lighthouse at Darling Park – an upcoming Henning Larsen project – which sprawls over a freeway that currently acts as a barrier between Sydney's urban centre and the waterfront. The idea is to create a village-like atmosphere: a 10,000-square-metre civic-hang-zone-slash-public-park. The Sydney Daily Telegraph is already calling it one of the "biggest slices of public land in the heart of the city in more than a century." Melbourne's Federation Square, built in 2002, had similar ambitions.

Due to be completed in 2028, Lighthouse at Darling Park is an example of what Maya calls 'human sustainability'. It's the bit on the Venn Diagram where 'urban design' and 'social well-being' overlap.

"Human sustainability in architecture is about designing environments that not only support people's *physical* well-being, but also nurture mental and emotional health. This involves acknowledging the complexity and diversity of human needs and moving beyond merely functional access to consider how people actually *feel* in a space," says Maya.

"As we navigate an era defined by technological mediation and diminished face-to-face interactions, architects have an opportunity – and a responsibility – to design spaces that create subtle forms of connection."

This is where public health, government policy, urban planning, psychology and architecture kind of bleed into one another. And Lighthouse at Darling Park is just one example. New York's High Line – a former elevated railway-turned public park, inspired by the Coulée Verte in Paris – has been a community-driven sensation, drawing over eight million visitors each year and re-energising the west side of Manhattan. BedZED in London – the UK's first dedicated zero-carbon community – made waves for encouraging neighbours to share communal laundry facilities, gardens and car-free spaces. And Copenhagen's Superkilen is the city's so-called "quality of life oasis": an urban park that integrates design elements from over 60 nationalities, including playgrounds, picnic areas, chess tables and open plazas.

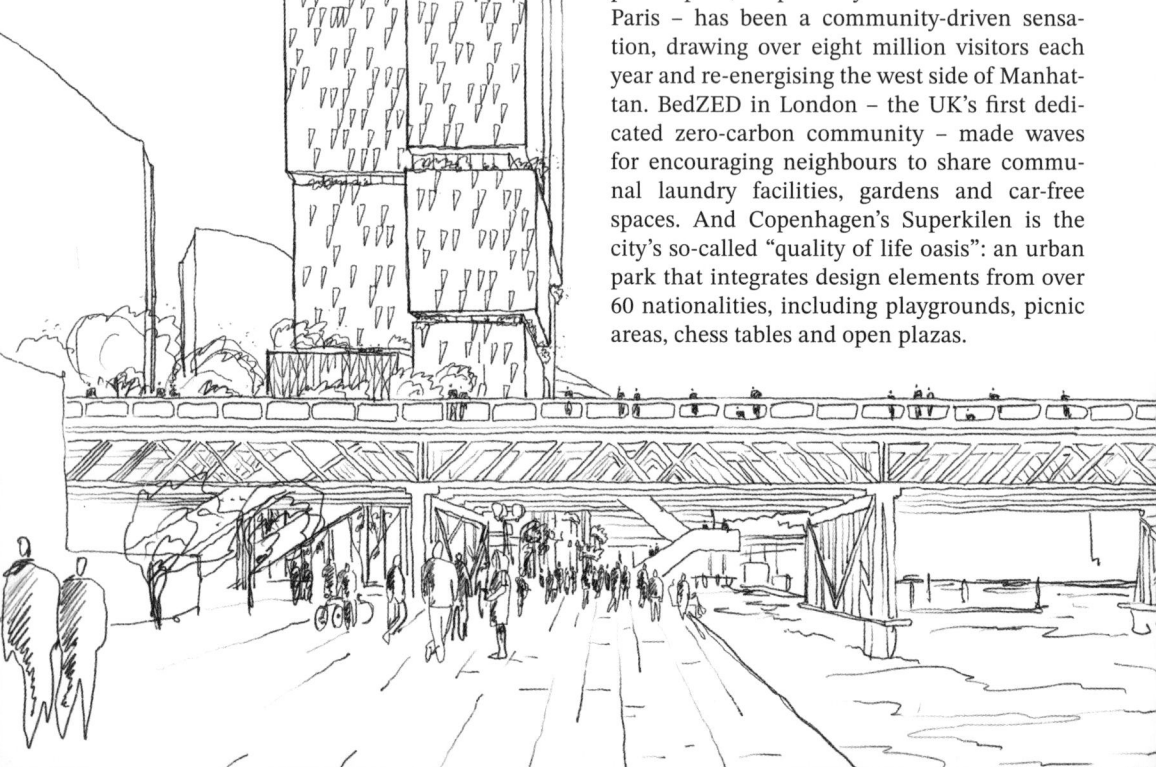

(Bottom left, Above)
Henning Larsen's project sketches for the Lighthouse at Darling Park detail how the spaces will promote connections between individuals and communities. Image courtesy of Henning Larsen Public Media Library.

When governments and architects work together, good things can happen. But as Maya says, good design on its own can't solve loneliness. Architects can encourage social interaction, but they don't have much say over meaningful *connection*, and when it comes to fighting loneliness, connection is really the secret sauce. Unfortunately, the thing about connection is that it tends to happen organically. You can't force it or legislate it; all you can do is make space for it to grow. It's like happiness in that respect. You can't manufacture genuine social connection, any more than you can *make* a society happy. Connection comes from the inside out, not the outside in. It's something else, something deeper, something hard to define – but we know it when we see it. It's something to do with purpose, joy, community, responsibility and self-sacrifice.

"What governments *can* do is implement policies that help everyone," Dr Lim says. "For example, we tax sugary drinks to disincentivise people from drinking them and help fight obesity. So how do we implement a *broad* solution for the population, one that will encourage people to have the time and space to develop meaningful social connections?"

This is the big question. But to answer it, we might need to start thinking smaller, rather than bigger; to step away from sardine-stacked cities for a minute, and journey to the little English market town of Frome, Somerset. Population: 28,000. In 2018, Frome (pronounced FROOM) became the epicentre for one of the most significant medical breakthroughs of the last 50 years. In short, the people of Frome may have found a cure for loneliness.

2 Architectural Determinism is a somewhat-debunked social theory that gained traction in the 1950s and 1960s, thanks to figures like Le Corbusier and the Bauhaus movement. The basic idea was that architecture could shape emotions and actions, often with the goal of getting people to *do* something (i.e. work harder, concentrate better, buy more stuff). Critics in the 1970s called it simplistic, but if you've ever walked out of a supermarket with a trolley full of unnecessary chocolate, you'll know there's some truth there.

The story began in 2013, when a local GP, Dr Helen Kingston, launched the Compassion Frome Project. Fed up with the incessant medicalisation of her patients – the way the system treated them as a collection of disconnected symptoms, rather than people – Dr Kingston teamed up with the NHS and Frome council to build a directory of agencies and community groups. She then employed 'health connectors' and voluntary 'community connectors' to link patients up with the relevant support networks. In practice, this could be anything from men's sheds to a financial service to driving someone to choir practice. It's been known for a while that sick people are at higher risk of isolation, and therefore loneliness, and it was hoped that by literally *prescribing* social interaction – just like any other medication – Dr Kingston and her colleagues could break the cycle.

A few years later, the data was analysed, and Frome became an overnight international sensation (at least among clinical psychologists and social policy wonks). While emergency hospital admissions across Somerset rose by 29 per cent during the three years of the study, in Frome they dropped 17 per cent. This wasn't just significant, it was unprecedented. As Julian Abel, a palliative physician and lead author of the study, said: "No other interventions on record have reduced emergency admissions across a population."

By prescribing targeted social remedies, Frome had somehow managed to shrink hospital admissions across their most at-risk population: sick people. By 2023, this 'social prescribing' model was being rolled out in 24 countries around the world, from Europe to Australia.

"There are dozens of trials going on," Dr Lim says. "In Australia, the Victorian state government has even implemented social prescribing for people with mental ill health and older adults. But the trick is finding a model that's *specific to each city* – because we know that community interaction differs from place to place."

Of course, we don't have to wait for governments, or even doctors, to prescribe social interaction, and some of the most successful anti-loneliness programs are the ones that have sprouted organically. From local communities. In Paris, for example, the wonderfully-named Republic of Super Neighbours has transformed the social fabric of the 14th arrondissement – a largely residential district on the Seine's Left Bank – with dozens of community meetups, local lunches and post-work drinks. No invitation necessary. The organisers have even set up 40 WhatsApp groups, where residents can get hyper-local assistance with everything from finding a cat sitter to fixing a broken toaster.

The Republic's founder, Patrick Bernard, says that we've got urban policy back-to-front. Instead of thinking large-scale, with sweeping legislative changes, we should be focussing on "the most local entity in a city": the neighbourhood.

"Urban strategy must focus on these micro-neighbourhoods, or three-minute villages, as I like to call them," Patrick told the *New York Times*, "Conviviality is a richness that is sleeping. When we awaken the sense of place and community, the citizens and urban fabric are transformed."

In a way, this is how most cities first started – outlying towns and villages simply got absorbed into the urban sprawl. In the old days, a Parisian might have only ever *seen* 10 per cent of Paris. To them, Paris was their arrondissement, their neighbourhood, their *street*. The smaller the social units get, the more meaningful and helpful they become. When you need a cup of sugar, you're not calling the mayor, are you?

What Frome and the Republic of Super Neighbours have really uncovered is the long-forgotten value of Community, in the capital C sense of the word. The rise of loneliness coincides with the atrophy of community, and everything that came with it: reciprocal care, a social safety net, over-the-fence gossip, charity, parochial pride, and the reassuring feeling that someone out there actually gives a shit. We traded a lot of this for streamlined convenience and intergalactic communication and next-day delivery and high-density living, but the price was secret – and significant. We lost the mysterious alchemy that turned strangers into neighbours, neighbours into friends, friends into loved ones.

Photographer Paul Kessler understands this, which is perhaps why *Solitary* hits so hard. Society has gained a lot over the last 50 years, but at what cost?

"I think that urban environments exacerbate isolation and loneliness," he says. "And yes, photography was a wonderful antidote to loneliness during COVID – photography has always been an antidote to loneliness and isolation as I age. But really, the friends I've made through my photography are way better than my photographs."

True Believers (2015)

wings (2014)

Drummer Girl (2016)

Q-Train (2019)

Waitress (2012)

Apollo (2018)

Meet Paul Kessel:

a photographer who distills street scenes into intimate and painterly frame-filled portraits. Candid by nature, his photography works on you like a brilliant piece of music – it's appealing from the outset but the more time you spend with it, the more the layers reveal themselves and suddenly, you're entranced. Paul turned to photography a month shy of his 70th birthday and has since exhibited his work in more than 200 shows, including five solo exhibitions. As a longtime New Yorker, the city and its people dependably rise to reward Paul's keen eye and patience as an inexhaustible source of colour, action and interest.

Interview Elizabeth Price
Images Paul Kessel

Some might say you've come to street photography late in life. How did it all start?

I always had a latent interest in photography but except for keeping a camera in a drawer, I rarely acted on it. Shortly after my daughter graduated college, she began working in photography. That stimulated my interest. At the same time, I retired from a career in psychology and because of age and injury, I stopped playing golf (I was an avid competitive golfer for over 50 years). Then when my daughter moved into her own apartment, I was at a loss about how to spend my time. Mostly on a last-minute whim, I wandered into the International Center of Photography, not far from where I lived in New York City, and that became my home base for more than 10 years of nonstop classes.

Initially, I focused on portraits and after a few years discovered street photography, which has been my major activity for about 15 years now. Even most of my dreams involve photography and a frequent nightmare is coming across a magnificent scene and my shutter button will not engage. (No interpretations please.) I became truly addicted to searching for interesting scenes and yearn to shoot all the time.

Do you draw any links between your former career in psychology and your current occupation as a street photographer? Any transferable skills?

I don't think there are significant links between my former career as a clinical psychologist and practicing street photography. Of course, both involve an interest in people, but beyond that, no meaningful links strike me. There is more of a connection between street photography and golf. I won't get into such connections here except to say that I treat street photography as a sport.

What's your ratio of forgettable shots to gems? How do you improve your chances of capturing a gem?

The ratio of "forgettable" shots to "gems" is huge. For myself it is something like 5000:1. Realistically, there may be three to five outstanding photos per year, many failures, and many 'okay' photos as well. The very best street photographers get exceptional pictures more often, but built into street photography is lots of failure. That is why it can become so addictive. I guess there is a connection with my former profession. Intermittent reinforcement is a powerful motivator. I remember learning that. I also know that the quest is more important than the success. But, the best way to achieve more good photos is to be out shooting as much as possible.

New York City is a consistent character in your work. What makes your hometown so photogenic in your eyes?

I believe that anything can be photogenic when in the right light. Probably awareness of light is right up there with making the most of good luck. Most of my photos are in New York City and, over time, one becomes aware of the nature of light in familiar areas. Additionally, I care as much about context as people in the photo.

You have such a painterly eye. Are you drawn to such scenes and compositions?

I have never before been told that my photos are "painterly". If indeed they are, it is largely luck. Luck plays more of a role in street photography than most other kinds of photography. That is primarily because many variables cannot be predicted or controlled. Perhaps one way to describe candid street photography is having the ability to make the most of good luck when it happens.

paulkessel.com

COLOUR CHEAT SHEET

INTERVIEW WITH RACHEL LACY BY ELIZABETH PRICE

If the walls of your home (like mine and many others) are painted a shade of white, brace yourself. What you're about to read contains some hard truths and strong opinions, albeit alongside some generous hand-holding if you want to embrace colour more wholeheartedly within the walls of your home. I learnt a huge amount during my very fun conversation with Haymes Paint Colour Lead, Rachel Lacy. I learned that the white walls in my home were not my own but were simply 'inherited'. A question waiting to be answered if you will. And I learnt a lot about colour in small spaces too. Spoiler alert: the answer is not always white.

"I think there's a myth – and it's definitely a myth – that painting a small space white makes it appear bigger. There's not a single logical principle that you can apply to that idea. It's still a small space. It's just white."

In fact, Rachel thinks painting a small space white can even have the opposite to the intended effect – by drawing even more attention to its smallness.

"One doesn't have to go all the way to a jewel tone (or whatever language one wants to use for a highly saturated colour), but I just wouldn't start with white. It's not going to do what you think it's going to do."

OK, so stretching ourselves beyond the safe and familiar territory of white is worthwhile. Noted. What else should we think about when working with colour and painting our small spaces and homes, Rachel?

1.

The new neutrals

Keeping a palette neutral is fine. Just remember that it doesn't need to be white. Pale greens, soft terracottas and blues are a great alternative and will behave better, especially if your space suffers from low light (more on this below). If a lot of your space is in shadow (as is often the case with small homes and apartments) a white space actually becomes a grey space.

But if you're deciding to add colour, it doesn't have to be all or nothing. There's so much between highly saturated colours and whites that you can do beautiful things with. These days those sagey greens are pretty much a neutral. (When I was a kid, neutrals were beige versions of beige). And you can do a lot with something like that – it's sort of hard to go wrong and the room will always feel better if it's that sagey green or a beautiful soft slightly muddy blue. It's just more interesting.

Soft neutrals at play in *Alaska Buildings* apartment in London designed by Studio 29 Architects Ltd. Image: Tarry + Perry.

(Top right) The palette in *Billinghurst* apartment in Buenos Aires reflects the creative and colourful energy of its residents. Designed by MoobArq. Image: MoobArq.

(Above) The enveloping bedroom in *Stroboscope* designed by studiobravo in Paris. Image: Bertrand Noël.

2.

Consider how and when you use the space.

If you're a working parent, like I've always been, then you are mostly in your bedroom at night. And I like the dark seductiveness of a darker bedroom. Thinking about the light in the room and the activity in the room helps to determine the depth of colour that you want to go to.

If you're home during the day throughout the week, a darker colour could just get a little bit heavy day in day out. But if you, like me and many others, are really only home in the evening and the weekends, you get a different level of exposure. I think that our life does travel in these chunks.

3.

Take ownership of your space

Having the freedom to paint your space is really important. I think it's difficult when people can't do that. But even when I lived in rentals, we still painted them. We just painted it when we left to return it to its original colour. Most paint companies now do a single coat white paint that covers most colours easily. And it really is worth it because it makes it your space. We've all lived places that are not ideal – that aren't quite what we want – and we make do. But when you get to live in the place that you love and you've made it what you want it to be, it will give you a kick every day.

Paint is one of the cheapest, most cost-effective ways to transform your space. It's pretty egalitarian. If you don't want to pay for painting, you can do it yourself. It's not complicated. People like to make painting sound complicated, but it's really not. It's actually reasonably hard to screw up.

(Right)

Interior designer Sara Leonor's colourful transformation of a bedroom in a mansion block apartment in London's Kings Cross. Image: Anna Batchelor.

(Left)

Tree House apartment in Hong Kong designed by Dennis Lo. Image: Dennis Lo Designs.

4.

Don't panic about the pressure of perfect

A lot of people panic and fall back to white due to the worry that they'll get it wrong or get sick of the outcome if they go with a colour, but when people can take the time to test and carefully consider (pointers below) the route they want to take with colour, the reward is just so enormous.

And it doesn't have to be a forever thing. So you don't have to think, 'my God, what I want to do at 30 still has to be relevant for how I want to live at 60'... because there is a lot of time in your life between those two periods to repaint your space!

Pretty in Pink in Athens designed by MoY studio. Image: Nikos Alexopoulos.

5.

Sample pots, sample pots, sample pots

Sample pots are by far the best way to go in order to try colours in different spaces – and in different areas of a space – to see where the lights hits. You can see how you like it – how you like living with it – and that does take time. Making the effort with test pots is so crucial because a lot of paint shop collateral is printed, which means it's not the actual paint. So painting a section of a surface is still the best way to test it in your room.

(Below)

Soft greens and dark greens feature throughout *401e* in Singapore designed by Knock Knock Studio. Image: Marcus Lim.

6.

Keep the palette simple

If you're planning a paint job, the only caveat is that a lot of colours don't work hugely well in small spaces. So if you've got a small space it's important to keep your palette quite simple. Monochromatic schemes work really well. If you've got architectural details you want to highlight, you can just use a full strength, or double strength of the same colour. And what that does is it just gives the room a little bit of movement without introducing a lot of different elements.

There's also a trend where you use a single colour (now called 'colour drenching' – but honestly, it's been around forever). Obviously, you use different products because you'll use a different product on your door and on your walls than you will on your ceiling. But you use the same colour and paint all the elements in that colour. It's incredibly easy to do. It can also take some of the anxiety away about thinking about what colours go well together.

7.

Zone your space with colour

Zoning with colour in a small space is a brilliant idea. It just takes a bit of courage because often there isn't an easy place to cut or divide a wall in a small apartment, but you also don't have to do it in a straight line. Something I love is working on the diagonal. The diagonal on a room is your longest view, so painting in a colour that recedes, then extends the longest view in the room. Pinterest will just give you so many examples of how to do that. The absence of a direct delineation or an architectural element that makes that easy doesn't mean you can't do it.

(Above)

A distinct shift in colour between spaces drives a sense of transition and shift in mood within *Project 26* in Singapore designed by Resistance. Image: form practice.

(Below)

Contrasting colours define the kitchen and dining areas within *Casa Triana* in Seville designed by Studio Noju. Image: Studio Noju.

A dark kitchen within Melbourne's *Microluxe* designed by Studio Edwards is enhanced by custom lighting illuminating the ceiling above and floor below. Image: Fraser Marsden.

8.

Don't fight the light

Le Corbusier said don't fight the light. When thinking about your colour scheme, think about how you can accentuate what the light's doing in your space. This might mean painting lighter where the light is and darker where it's darker. Do what the light does. Colour is really impacted by light sources because colour is light. So, it's going to look different under different light sources, which is why test pots are such a good idea. So if a space is dark, maybe don't fight it within colour. Just get imaginative with lights

As small houses and apartments tend to be parts of bigger houses or buildings, there's a pretty good chance a fair amount of them are going to be in shadow. And if you're dealing with shadow, white's just going to look grey. Titanium dioxide is used to make paint white. It's also in sunscreen and it gives paint its opacity and its whiteness. It used to be incredibly cheap but now it's expensive and the further you grind it, the bluer it goes. So you'll find that a lot of whites now have a slightly blue-grey undertone. As a result, a white room in the evening will be very grey in the corners. It's weird to me. Everyone paints their houses white, but their Instagram feeds are full of coloured houses.

(Below)
Dramatic custom lighting elevates the moody colour and materials palette throughout *Microluxe* (designed by Studio Edwards). Image: Fraser Marsden.

9.

Consistency makes it feel cohesive

If you're keen to work with multiple colours, think about the strength of colour and the weight of colour you're using. You don't want to go from a deeply saturated room to a pale room. If you're going to go with a warm grey then you could have a beautiful sagey warm green and then a blue, but keep them of a similar weight so that there's this sort of gentle movement through the spaces and a sense of consistency so it's not like 'Whoa! Whoa! Whoa!'. You just want to make sure that when you have your palette, that even if they're in different parts of your home and they're not next to each other, that you keep colour in your mind's eye. So, you want it to have a cohesive feel. You want the colours to feel that they could all be next to each other, even if they aren't.

(Above)

A soft, calming palette dominates throughout *Villa Montserrat* in Barcelona. Designed by furniture designer Max Enrich and his partner Diana Martin. Image: Never Too Small.

(Below)

A cohesive colour palette defines *Kloedenstraße* in Berlin designed by Dax I. Image: Wolfgang Stahr.

10.

Don't discount brown

Browns have such a bad reputation, which is such a shame because they're so easy to live with. Those beautiful warm umbers that Le Corbusier had in his palette are so beautiful and versatile. You can put anything against them. But everyone has this kind of 70s-brown bee in their bonnet. There's a huge amount of that rich red earthy terracotta around, which I completely love, and the fact that Laminex recently put out that 'Kalamata' range is testament to the general acceptance that browns are beautiful colours and they have been for a really long time.

The home of architect Maddie Sewall within *Skye House* – part of the award-winning Nightingale Village in Melbourne. Maddie was the lead architect on the project with Breathe Architecture. Image: Dylan James.

Rachel, a friend of Maddie's, advised her that the apartment "needed to be brown". Image: Dylan James.

"Slightly muddy off-centre colours" that are "blue to one person and green to another" within *Kloedenstraße* in Berlin designed by Dax I. Image: Wolfgang Stahr.

11.

Consider 'chameleon colours'

I think you have to be very brave and confident to use bright saturated colours as opposed to the more muted tones. The colours that sit on the edge of each colour group are always the most beautiful to me. I love those colours that are blue to one person and grey to another or green to one and blue to another. They just slightly shift. I think those slightly muddy off-centre colours are the easiest colours to use and the most forgiving and they look different under different light too. They are fractionally harder to choose because you really need to use that sample pot, paint it up, sit with it for a while and see what it's like in the changing light of day and under your artificial lights, but it will be worth it.

12.

Harness recessive colours

If you think of Yves Klein's 'International Klein Blue' made with the ultramarine pigment, that colour recedes. For Le Corbusier, if there was a hallway, he might paint one wall with ultramarine blue and he might paint a stair balustrade with umber because umber makes objects disappear. So, thinking about how you use colour generally: cooler colours recede and warmer colours advance. So, red, for example, is a terrible colour to use on the floor because it comes up at you. It's a good colour if you've got an incredibly long room or a hallway and you want the end wall to have the sense of advancing towards you. That's loosely how they work. So if you want objects or walls or balustrades or elements to sit back and to become less visible, umber and soft browns are a really good choice.

The home of architect Maddie Sewall in Melbourne, designed by Maddie and Breathe Architecture. Image: Dylan James.

(Above) Colourful cabinetry, furniture, books and artwork do the heavy lifting in mone studio's *Darley Studio* in Sydney. Image: Never Too Small.

(Below) A gallery wall adds colour and interest in *401e* in Singapore designed by Knock Knock Studio. Image: Marcus Lim.

(Above)

A glossy blue resin paint inspired by Persian indigo coats the bathroom surfaces in *Urban Cabin* designed by Francesca Perani. Image: Francesca Perani.

13.

Play with colour without paint

There's a tonne of fun you can have with color that doesn't involve painting walls. Joinery, furniture, tiles, vases – and even plates – they don't have to be white. (God help us!).

WHEN DESIGN MET COLOUR

WORDS PENNY CRASWELL

We humans have long understood the symbolic and emotive powers of colour. Colour holds meaning, drives memories and stirs emotions. And yet, an interest in welcoming colour – especially vivid colour – into our homes, is a relatively modern condition. It would take a brave bastion of designers who dared to join the ranks of "savage nations, uneducated people, and children…" to coax us out of our domestically chromophobic ways.

Savage nations, uneducated people, and children have a great predilection for vivid colors.
– Johann Wolfgang von Goethe, 1810

The ancient Greeks didn't have a word for blue. For them, the colour spectrum ranged from light to dark, with white at one end and black at the other. Yellow was a little darker than white and blue was a little lighter than black. The words for colour in Greek literature are often confusing – the "wine-dark" sea is a good example. If not blue, I can see calling the sea green, or grey. But wine-dark?[1] In ancient Rome, Tyrian purple was so valuable that by law it was only worn by magistrates, royals and generals. It also gave off a huge stink, made from crushed sea snails and was incredibly expensive – 10,000 crushed snails, cooked for a week, only made 1 gram of dye. Weirdly, even though we know Tyrian purple was, uh, purple, Pliny the Elder[2] described it as having: "a greenish hue".

In fact, the names of colours are not as straightforward as we think. And the words we use can have a huge effect on how we see them. For us, the basic primary colours – red, yellow, blue – and secondaries – orange, green and purple – are joined by those, not nearly so fun, brown, black and white. Pink is an interesting one – and not a colour at all in some languages. Japanese doesn't have a word for pink, just the hyphenated word *momo-iro* which literally means "peach blossom colour". In other languages it's just called light-red. And, in Italian, there is an extra word for light blue that we do not have in English: *azzurro*. The same is true in French, Albanian, Hebrew and Russian. Then there's "orange", which in Irish is *flannbhuí*, meaning "blood yellow". And in Hungarian there are two words for red *piros* and *vörös*, with *vörös* meaning dark red.

(Left)

Although the original design of Rietveld's Red and Blue Chair was produced in 1918, the chair's colour scheme of distinctive primary colours and black painted frame (as we still know it today) was later applied in 1923.

1 The references to colour in ancient Greek texts are so haphazard that one 19th century politician went so far as to claim that Greeks must have been colour blind. But this is not the case – references to colour were confusing in other ancient languages too – a decade later one scholar found the same muddled references to colour in the Koran, the Bible, ancient Chinese stories and Icelandic sagas. For more detail, check out Kassia St Clair's book *The Secret Lives of Colour*, which also charts the origin and history of 70 different shades from saffron to fuchsia, vermilion to mauve, and ultramarine to celadon.

2 Pliny the Elder was an ancient Roman whose encyclopedic works were considered an authority on scientific matters until the Middle Ages.

All of this has an impact on what we see. As does colour theory, a method of colour analysis used in both art and design. Bauhaus colour theorist Johannes Itten believed that different colours are associated with different emotions. Itten called an individual's colour preferences their 'subjective colours' – he described one of his students as "light violet, light blue, blue-gray, yellow, white and a touch of black" with a fundamental tone that was "hard, cold and somewhat brittle"[3] – no doubt he was the life of the party. He also had a hunch that colours could have a big impact on our moods. However, while colour theory was taught at the Bauhaus by Itten[4], and also by Wassily Kandinsky, Paul Klee and Josef Albers, the use of colour in furniture and object design was still relatively rare in this time – two of the most famous Bauhaus designs, the Barcelona chair by van der Rohe and the Wassily chair by Marcel Breuer, were famously black and chrome.[5]

The truth is that for the longest time, the history of design, and especially furniture, was stuck in varying tones of timber, a lot of it dark and heavy. It wasn't until the 20th century that brightly-coloured furniture was even really made, let alone commonplace. One of the first iconic pieces of design history to really use colour in an interesting way was the Red and Blue chair by Gerrit Rietveld from 1923. Rietveld was part of the Dutch De Stijl movement, an art movement made famous by the geometric coloured works of Piet Mondrian. The chair's form, and its colour, conform to Rietveld's manifesto of Neoplasticism, in which the basic elements of the chair – seat, back, arms, legs – have been simplified into intersecting planes. Its colours have also been distributed this way – red for the back, blue for the seat, and black for the arms and connecting elements (with a touch of yellow on their ends). The use of primary colours on separate planes represented a turn away from nature, towards the machine age. It presents a totally modern form. "It is interesting just how little importance was given to the application or integration of colour into domestic objects prior to World War I," writes David Harrison in *A Century of Colour in Design*. "It was the De Stijl movement … that kickstarted the use of primary colours."

But there was one material that would inject bright, vivid colour into our homes – and particularly furniture and household objects – plastic. A wonder material, it was everything modern: new, cheap and fun. And it was colourful. The first type of plastic to become ubiquitous in our homes – Bakelite – was used in telephones, radios, kitchenware, light switches and toys, with global production at about 178,000 tonnes by 1944. Fibreglass began to be used in furniture from the 1950s with the Eames fibreglass chair. But the most important innovation for the development of plastic furniture was polypropylene, which went into production in the early 1950s. This mass-produced, colourful and cheap material was perfect for the age of consumerism and pop design.[6] Danish designer Verner Panton's chair, eponymously called the Panton chair, released in 1967, epitomises this new era of plastic design and freedom to express yourself in full colour.

> "The main purpose of my work is to provoke people into using their imagination," Panton said. "Most people spend their lives housed in dreary, grey-beige conformity, mortally afraid of using colours."

Designers of this era made full use of these new materials and technologies to inject colour into our lives, and there were no designers more dedicated to colour than the Italians. Gaetano Pesce's Up chair and ottoman, Vico Magistretti's Eclisse lamp, Anna Castelli Ferrieri's Componibili storage tables, Ettore Sottsass's Olivetti Valentine typewriter, Achille and Pier Giacomo Castiglioni's Snoopy lamp – these are icons of design writ in bold oranges, reds, blues and greens. Red in particular is notable in Italian design, a fact that Kendrah Morgan, curator of

---

3 Interestingly, Itten's theory was one of the earliest precursors to modern colour theory in fashion and beauty, in which you may be classified as an autumn, winter, spring or summer.
4 Itten's colour star, consisting of six concentric circles and 12 meridians was published in 1921.
5 A notable exception is the Nesting tables by Josef Albers from 1926, in which each tabletop has a different Bauhaus colour – white, yellow, orange and blue.
6 Interestingly, one more ingredient helped colour to really take off as an idea in interiors, and that is colour printing in magazines and, specifically, colour advertising. The introduction of plastic, the lowering cost of household goods and the advent of glossy colour magazines created a perfect storm and the response was huge.

Valentine Portable Typewriter by Ettore Sottsass and Perry King for Olivetti, 1968

Long before he founded Memphis Milano, Ettore Sottsass, designed The Valentine Portable Typewriter along with British designer Perry King for Italian manufacturer Olivetti. Introduced on Valentine's day 1969, the Valentine Portable Typewriter was one of the earliest and most iconic plastic-bodied typewriter designs, with its signature red colour and matching plastic case. Turning to Pop Art, Sottsass drew inspiration from artist Tom Wesselman's nudes featuring pink breasts and orange nipples for the typewriter's bright orange scroll caps. Although its design was distinctive and was popular amongst design circles, the Valentine unfortunately didn't reach mass audiences. It does, however, still remain an icon of Italian design; featuring in various permanent collections, including the Metropolitan Museum of Art, London's Design Museum and the Powerhouse Museum in Sydney.

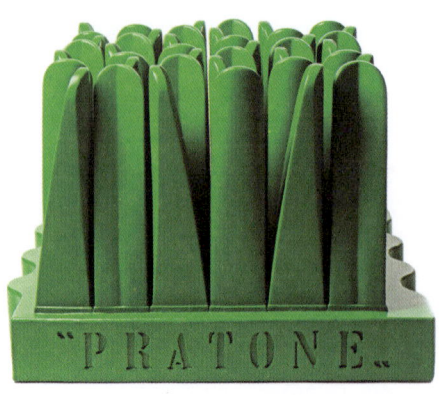

7.

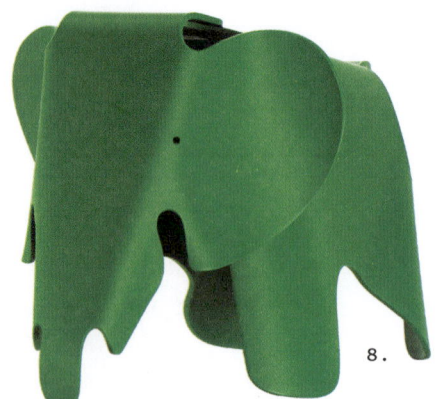

8.

9.

10.

11.

12.

Another Green Cactus® by Guido Drocco and Franco Mello for Gufram, 1972

Sculptural, spongy, emerald green and irrefutably cheerful, the Gufram Cactus is an icon of Italian design that was originally released in 1972. Designed by Guido Drocco and Franco Mello on a cold winter's day in Turin, it speaks of deserts, sun and heat and is an emblematic example of the Italian Radical Design movement, which sought to break free from design norms and present new, provocative and unexpected forms. And so, even though it is a useable hat stand, it transcends its use, presenting us with a completely original form – perky and soft to the touch. The Cactus is made by casting polyurethane foam in a mould, a new process at the time of its release. Interestingly, each of the four arms are made in a separate mould from the trunk, then the whole is assembled and finished by hand, before being spraypainted in green. The Guflac paint used was developed by Gufram and ensures that the finish is vibrant but with a flexible skin. Gufram is also famous for the production of the Bocca sofa, which is made in the shape of Mae West's lips, and the Pratone, another green sculptural design that looks like a dozen blades of oversized plastic grass on a square (and is actually a seat).

Ball Chair by Eero Aarnio, 1963

The Ball Chair is one of the most famous designs of the 20th century and is most iconic in its orange form. Designed in 1963, it was the brainchild of Finnish designer Eero Aarnio who, after having discovered the possibilities of fibreglass, envisioned a chair in the shape of a ball that would enclose the top half of the body like a cocoon. Fibreglass had been around for a few decades but was mainly used in boating until the 1950s - even then it had patents that made it expensive to work with. By the time Aarnio designed the Ball chair those patents had expired, and the ball shape and bright colour of the chair was directly inspired by the material's strength, malleability, glossy smooth finish and ability to hold vivid hues. In terms of colours, the designer preferred a limited number of bright saturated colours. The Ball Chair was an instant hit when introduced in 1966 and featured in films including: *The Italian Job, Mars Attacks!* and *Dazed and Confused*.

**Vermelha chair
by Campana Brothers for Edra, 1993**

Brazilian designers and brothers Fernando and Humberto Campana designed the Vermelha chair in 1993, a chair made of 450 metres of soft thick red rope that is piled and woven onto its frame, with the spaghetti-like excess acting as padding. The name - Vermelha - Portuguese for 'red' - comes from the Latin *vermiculus* or 'little worm' which refers to the Kermes vermilio insect, which since Neolithic times has been crushed to make the colour vermilion or crimson. In an interview, Humberto described the chair as a homage to Brazil: "The Vermelha chair is an homage to chaos," says Humberto. "It's a portrait of Brazil, a melting pot of culture and races ... and I try to manifest this idea into a kind of chair that is chaotic in its very construction." Originally created as an art piece, the chair was only made and sold a few times in its first five years before catching the eye of Italian brand Edra's creative director Massimo Morozzi who put the chair into production. Although the chair is now made commercially, it is still woven by hand and requires several days' work by a single person with expertise in Brazilian weaving.

(fold-out)
1. Butter Stool by Gibson Karlo for DesignByThem (2011). 2. Snoopy Table Lamp by Achille & Pier Giacomo Castiglioni (1967). 3. Flowerpot VP9 by Verner Panton for &Tradition (1969). 4. Big Friendly by CJ Anderson for Dowel Jones (2020). 5. Ekstrem™ chair by Terje Ekstrøm for Varier (1984). 6. Goblet Planter by Cindy Lee-Davies for Lightly (2018). 7. Pratone® by Giorgio Ceretti, Pietro Derossi and Riccardo Rosso for Gufram (1971). 8. Eames Elephant by Charles and Ray Eames for Vitra (1945). 9. Bridges by Muller Van Severen for Barcelona Design (2024). 10. Stacking Chair by Verner Panton for Vitra (1967). 11. Sparkling Chair by Marcel Wanders for Magis (2010). 12. Quilt Sofa by Ronan and Erwan Bouroullec for Established & Sons (2009). 13. Rey Chair by Bruno Rey for Hay and Dietiker (1971). 14. Bell Lamp by Tom Dixon (2012). 15. Componibili by Anna Castelli Ferrieri for Kartell (1967). 16. Spun chair by Thomas Heatherwick for Magis (2010). 17. Bocca® by Studio 65 for Gufram (1970). 18. Bellhop by Edward Barber and Jay Osgerby for Flos (2017). 19. Float by Luca Nichetto for La Chance (2012). 20. Showtime Vases by Jaime Hayon for Barcelona Design (2006). 21. Bishop Stool by India Mahdavi (1999). 22. Tip Ton by Edward Barber and Jay Osgerby for Vitra (2009). 23. Eclisse by Vico Magistretti for Artemide (1965). 24. Panthella Lamp by Verner Panton for Louis Poulsen (1971).

the *Molto Bello: Icons of Modern Italian Design* exhibition at Heide Museum, Melbourne, partially attributes to an expression of national identity. "In the exhibition, a lot of the objects are bright red, and we often associate red with Italian design," she says. "With the emergence of plastics, the range of colours increased. They became more vibrant and saturated because of new technologies around plastics and the use of dyes. This was in the 1950s and 60s when Italy was becoming a mass consumer society."

Italian design was also influenced heavily by the visual arts and by pop art. "In Italian design," says Kendrah, "those pop art hallmarks such as bold colours, repeated forms, everyday objects and imagery, irony and satire, all came out." In particular, the Valentine typewriter by Ettore Sottsass for Olivetti was iconic, the first all-plastic typewriter, designed not for boring office life, but for the writer or poet. "It is a literary, emotional object that Sottsass intended to be used, for example, by a poet out in the landscape, in a beautiful, inspirational setting," says Kendrah. The orange scroll caps were directly inspired by the nipples of a nude in a painting by pop artist Tom Wesselmann.

Italian design continued to dominate, especially in the development of coloured furniture and design, for decades, through the swinging sixties and into the orange and brown of the 1970s. By the 1980s, colour use had shifted, with postmodern pastiche heralding an era of anything goes. The Memphis Milano collective (see p36) embraced new materials and colour combinations, and Miami Vice inspired interiors in beige with teal, pink, peach or neon accents. But the era of colour stuttered out in the 1990s, when colour started to be abandoned in favour of chrome, glass and black furniture, clean lines and minimalism. It is from this point on that grey and other neutrals start to dominate in our homes, along with white, black, timber and other neutrals.

But it needn't be so. Eryca Green of Melbourne's Smith Street Bazaar is a huge lover of colour. "I deplore the current trend of varying stages of greys and beiges. I think colour can be a really emotive thing, and I personally am not afraid of it," she says. "I love the Memphis approach to colour and that irreverence." In her study, leaning against the wall, she has a Tahiti Table lamp by Memphis Milano, with its combined pink, yellow, brown and red. And on the table next to it, a Snoopy lamp by Achille Castiglione in green. "There is a black one, but the green is probably best known," she says. "That green is something I really love."

We've come a long way since 1810 then. In his *Theory of Colors* Goethe observed that "...people of refinement avoid vivid colours in their dress and the objects that are about them, and seem inclined to banish them altogether from their presence." And yet the era of domestic chromophobia is far from over: 'millennial grey' and 'sad beige' still dominate our homes and offer a calming refuge for many. But will they ever make our hearts sing? Some designers, like Denmark's Raw Color (see p210) and Studio RENS in the Netherlands, think not and in the case of the latter, describe themselves as "colourful to the core" with colour driving their entire design process. Iranian-born Paris-based architect and designer India Mahdavi is also an advocate of living with colour. She told *Surface* magazine: "My work is about joy and sunshine and how you can change the mood of a room full of people when the place has some kind of happiness to it. People need colour. If I can bring that into the environments I create, I'm happy."[7]

[7] Other contemporary designers not afraid to work with colour include US-based Karim Rashid, Netherlands-based Hella Jongerius and UK-based Bethan Laura Wood.

The Everyday Architect

INTERVIEW ELIZABETH PRICE

Nestled in the heart of bustling Bangkok is a unique and unspoilt neighbourhood. The ancient structures of temples, mosques and churches punctuate rows of modest family homes. House fronts here are spaces to dry washing and cook meals amongst clustered collections of potted plants. It's a scene that might seem busy or even untidy to some, but to architect Chatchavan Suwansawat, it is a scene of perfect harmony – and one where creativity and ingenuity surprises and delights him daily.

(178-179)
Chatchavan Suwansawat and his Everyday Architecture Studio in Bangkok. Studio images: Ohm Anawat; Portrait image: Suwicha Pitakkanchanakul.

(Right)
Some of the images Chatchavan has captured of the ingenious creativity and resourcefulness to be found on the neighbourhood streets of Bangkok. Images: Chatchavan Suwansawat.

"I was born and raised in this area. A funny thing that a lot of my friends don't know is that as a child, I was raised in a very sheltered way. My parents never let me go outside to play with other kids in our neighborhood."

But the pull was strong. As Chatchavan grew up, exploring Bangkok – and especially his own neighbourhood of Somdej Chao Phraya – became his hobby and passion. His observations from these regular expeditions have fueled two books: *Architect-Jer* (the Thai word *jer* means 'find' or 'come across') and *365 Days of Thai Urban Mess Architecture* and he has based his architectural practice here – the Everyday Architect Design Studio.

We meet Chatchavan to unpack the complexities of destigmatising colourful architecture in Thailand and to learn why "street-level creativity and resourcefulness" is where designers should look to solve the pressing challenges of urban life and planning.

Let's start with colour. What significance does colour hold in Thai culture?

Most people in Thai society have a blend of beliefs between Buddhism and Hinduism. This hybrid belief system is also similar to neighbouring countries such as Myanmar, Laos and Cambodia, as these countries have a longstanding historical connection with Thailand. So most people in this region have beliefs related to stars, astronomy and astrology, which are part of the roots of Hinduism. For example, the names of the days of the week are derived from the names of celestial bodies, such as Monday - Moon, Tuesday - Mars. Each celestial body is likened to a deity found in mythological beliefs, and each deity is associated with a specific colour.[1]

As a result, those who still hold tightly to these traditional beliefs often try to align themselves with the corresponding colours for each day, particularly in choosing the colours of their clothing, to bring good luck each day. This concept of lucky colours may even extend to individual preferences; for instance, if you were born on a Thursday, you might be suited to the colour orange for your entire life. However, nowadays, people may be starting to believe less in these significant beliefs.

How has this cultural connection with colour played out in Thai architecture?

Historians have explored and noted that in ancient times, architecture in Thailand rarely used colours. The colours that appeared were often linked to details such as Chinese ceramics or gold lacquer applied to sculptures. As for actual paint products used for the architecture, they were likely influenced by Western architecture during the reign of King Rama IV (around 160 years ago) for the royal families' palaces and vacation houses. Pastel tones were dominant at that time, and the choice of colours in architecture continued to be adjusted and selected according to the preferences of the king and the upper class.

1   Monday (Moon) – Yellow; Tuesday (Mars) – Pink; Wednesday (Mercury) – Green; Thursday (Jupiter) – Orange; Friday (Venus) – Blue; Saturday (Saturn) – Purple; Sunday (Sun) – Red.

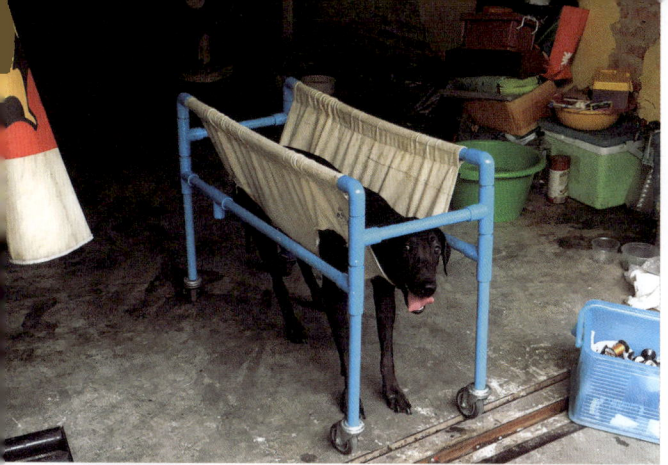

This has led to a frequent display of brightly coloured and striking buildings everywhere, especially in rural areas, where we often find homes painted in extremely vibrant colours, such as a green railing contrasting with a pink house, or a blue staircase alongside a green house with yellow pillars against a pink beam. These bright and vivid colours reflect the tastes of ordinary people in Thai society.

<u>What are your theories about where this attraction to such bold and clashing colours comes from? Does it relate back to the celestial bodies or is there something else at play?</u>

I have playfully analysed the reasons why ordinary Thai people tend to prefer such bright and striking colours and I identified three main reasons:

1. We did not grow up with an understanding of colour shades or tone control. When it comes to blue, there is no light blue or dark blue; there is only one bright blue paint available in the local store.

2. Thailand is a hot country and year-round sunlight can easily fade house paint colours. Choosing to paint in the brightest and most vivid colours is a way to save costs on repainting the house.

3. Lastly, it is still related to beliefs about luck. Since we are painting it ourselves, we must choose colours that align with our individual preferences (and beliefs) because the house is meant to last a lifetime.

DEITIES, DAYS & COLOURS

Colour	Day	Deity
🟡	MONDAY	MOON
🔴	TUESDAY	MARS
🟢	WEDNESDAY	MERCURY
🟠	THURSDAY	JUPITER
🔵	FRIDAY	VENUS
🟣	SATURDAY	SATURN
🔴	SUNDAY	SUN

As urban construction began to expand, colour regulations were only enforced in the early stages. Since then, paint products have become easily accessible to the people, reflecting the characteristics of a capitalist era. These days, there are not many laws regulating building colours in Thailand (except for some regulations in old towns).

(Left)
The "urban mess" that inspired the central design concept within Chatchavan's renovation of Din Daeng House (see pp 186-187).

(Right)
Some extracts from Chatchavan's *Thai Urban Mess Architecture* project – a collection of 365 sketches that document small objects and architectural designs created by everyday people on the streets of Bangkok from late 2019 to late 2020.

But there's some tension here about these choices not being *fashionable*, right?

Currently, there is a tendency – especially among architects and designers – to view the use of bright and vibrant colours in new architecture as a reflection of poor taste. Instead, they often choose colours based on internet trends, whether it be Western tonal shades or warm Japanese tones. Every time I open a design magazine in Thai, I find it contradicts the overall scenes of society. Whenever a house conceived by a designer appears in a community or neighbourhood, it often looks out of place and different from the surroundings, even if that house is painted in a monotone.

As an architect who is interested in everyday culture, I have come to realise that using vibrant colours in newly designed architecture is the answer to integrating new elements with our urban fabric and traditional communities. It is friendly and reduces disparities in architecture, and preserves the uniqueness and freedom of spirit of the people.

Why are you so passionate about this 'everyday culture'?

It originates from the writing of my two books. If you have ever visited Bangkok, you would have encountered the chaos that comes with the diversity and vibrancy of the people in this big city. I was born and have spent my entire life in Bangkok. My interests and inspirations in my work over the years are directly and inseparably connected to this city. I often choose to walk on weekends with excitement to explore the scenes of the city and its people, as well as to observe urban vernacular design from the locals who strive to continue living in a city that people both love and hate.

What do you do with these observations? Does this relate to your 'Thai Urban Mess' project?

Yes. The *Thai Urban Mess Architecture* project is a collection of 365 sketches that document small objects and architectural designs created by everyday people on the streets of Bangkok from late 2019 to late 2020. These sketches capture the street-level creativity and resourcefulness that often goes unnoticed by most Thai citizens. Many people fail to recognise the potential of these informal designs to inspire improvements in urban life and city planning. Through the process of sketching these designs for more than a year, I began to understand the hidden conditions and challenges of the city – issues that are also often overlooked. The solutions I encountered were marked by surprising creativity and ingenuity, consistently challenging the conventional thinking and perspectives of designers.

Three years after completing the collection, I spent time arranging and analysing the relationships between all the images, which eventually evolved into 13 articles. This body of work became the book *365 Days of Thai Urban Mess Architecture*.

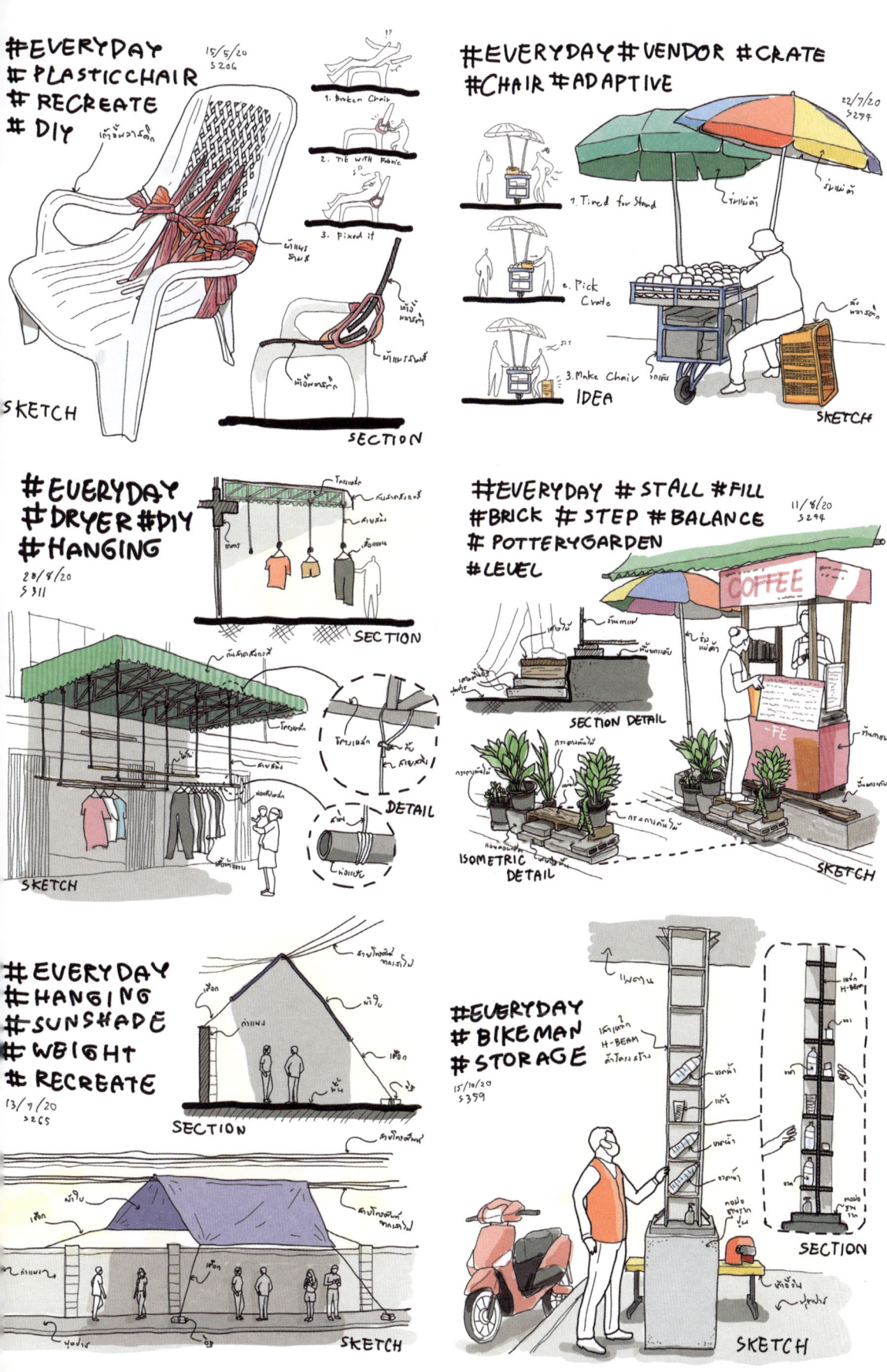

How did this project feed into the concepts and design for your recent renovation project, Din Daeng House?

The *Din Daeng House* is a 180-square-metre renovation project completed at the end of 2024 with a colour scheme of bold green and vibrant red (I gave my client complete freedom to choose these colours). The project was inspired by observing street vendors and stall owners utilising air-hanging techniques. They creatively repurposed pipes to hang items, maximising the use of limited space. This concept was integrated into the staircase handrails throughout the house, allowing the homeowner to organise belongings or hang clothes on any of the rails as needed. This hanging system takes up minimal space but is highly efficient, offering a more practical alternative to traditional built-in cabinets.

So clever. Can you tell us more about how you empower your clients when it comes to colour and rehabilitate their relationship with these vibrant hues?

To me, colour reflects the evolving tastes of society at any given time. It is also a universally understandable creative element, whether you are a designer, a street vendor or a local. On a deeper level, colour serves as one of the most powerful mediums for freedom of expression in architecture. It empowers individuals to make choices that reflect their personal beliefs or unique identity at an affordable cost. Because of this, I always give clients as much freedom as possible when it comes to colour in every architectural project. I help them find colours that represent themselves. At the same time, I aim to harmonise the colours with the surroundings, trying to enhance a sense of connection and unity within the community.

everydayarchitectdesignstudio.com

(Top left)
The original facade of Din Daeng House before Chatchavan's renovation of the home in 2024. Image: Chatchavan Suwansawat.

(Top right)
Storage was an obvious challenge that needed addressing with the redesign of Din Daeng House. Image: Chatchavan Suwansawat.

AFTER

(Left)
The vibrant red and teal that appear on the rejuvenated facade of Din Daeng House also appear inside the home. Image: Ohm Anawat.

(Above and below)
The street-vendor inspired design solution that underpins Din Daeng House proves to be both a space efficient and practical response to the resident's storage challenges. Images: Ohm Anawat.

Inspiration & ideas for colour & cleverness.

WORDS ELOÏSE LACHICORÉE

Image: Sirisak Chantorn courtesy of Kitt.Ta.Khon.

Jim Thompson x Kitt.Ta.Khon ARCHIPELAGO collection

We were immediately struck by the way colour elevates such a simple and common shape of stool with this collaboration between heritage Thai silk brand Jim Thompson and Thai furniture design studio Kitt.Ta.Khon. Designer Teerapoj Teeropas developed new weaving techniques for the collection to complement the fabric designs from Jim Thompson. The Takpha Chair, forming part of the ARCHIPELAGO collection, features an aluminium structural frame embellished with colourful hand-woven recycled plastic and a seat cushion upholstered in fabrics from Jim Thompson's outdoor range to make the handsome little stools friendly for indoors or out.

kitt-ta-khon.com

Images: Kanrapee Chokpaiboon courtesy of Kitt.Ta.Khon.

Images: Melissa Cowan courtesy of Into Carry.

Into Carry
Sexy bags and accessories from waste

Luke Phillips' circular design studio designs and makes bags and other adjacent accessories out of waste textiles and other materials like soft plastics. The Into Carry model is based on simple design templates that allow a vast range of low-value waste materials to be transformed into unique and useful things to carry other things in. Luke also empowers others to "upcycle like a pro" with in-person and online workshops, classes and courses. You too can learn how to turn your soy milk cartons, instant noodle wrappers and other waste into "durable, functional, sexy bags".

intocarry.co

Images courtesy of Hayon Studio.

Jaime Hayon
Multileg Collection

Designed for the 2006 Milano Furniture Fair, Spanish designer Jaime Hayon's Multileg collection for BD Barcelona features cabinets and tables in a range of shapes and sizes, with entirely customisable configurations of 12 differently-shaped and patterned legs. Ranging from minimal and geometric to more organic and sculptural shapes, the legs transform the otherwise simple pieces into something much more playful.

hayonstudio.com

INHABITING A HOUSE OF CRIMSON FLAMES

Loving and living within colour. Such is the experience of a couple who commissioned our friends at ATOMAA, in collaboration with architect Fabio Figaroli, to reimagine their Milanese apartment. And this is their love letter to the outcome: a home that constantly delights them with its chameleon-like charms while also feeling like it's always been theirs.

WORDS ANDREA AND FRANCESCA

(Below)

An architectural model of "the great protagonist of the living area...": a totem clad in an Ettore Sottsass veneer that features "...ready-to-transform geometries, unexpected spaces and openings...". Image: courtesy of ATOMAA.

(Right)

Many shades of blue also find their place throughout the 'House of Crimson Flames'. Images: Francesco Stelitano.

One of the things that brings us the most joy in life is colour. Pure colour, regardless of the object or material it adorns, and its juxtaposition – whether intentional or accidental, harmonious or clashing – with other colours, which instantly creates a unique visual universe to immerse ourselves in. We deal with colour in our work, but this little obsession follows us into our free time as well.

We often catch ourselves pausing without reason, for a comically long time, in front of particularly striking colour combinations. It happens to us like children gazing at shelves of pencils and markers in stores, looking at a beautiful poster on the street, or debating whether the car parked in front of us is "powder blue" or "grey with a hint of blue".

Every time we look around our new home, besides feeling grateful to Fabio, Cesare, Andrea, Umberto and their team for designing a space that is welcoming, functional, generous in space and varied in perspectives, we are delighted because together we created a place where colour is taken seriously. Every element of this house has its own chromatic identity and often expresses it with intense simplicity through a flat colour: the green of doors and cabinets, the blue of the guest bathroom, the greys of the walls of the service block, the deep purple resin flooring in the sleeping area.

Three elements are exceptions in this sense. The central reinforced concrete pillar, which, once freed for the first time in all its beauty, revealed, like a small archaeological operation, pencil inscriptions made by workers in 1966, which we made sure to preserve. The cement tile floor of the living area, which, despite being born of an innovative technique, reflects our love for a certain traditional 'Milanese' touch (which recurs in various other details): faced with the need to choose a combination of three colours, it was immediate for all of us to think of the yellow-black-and-white linoleum by Gio Ponti.

The third element that escapes the logic of flat colour is the great protagonist of the living area, the totem clad in veneer signed by Ettore Sottsass.

In this magical column, our home finds its climax, with minimalist yet ready-to-transform geometries, unexpected spaces and openings, and, naturally, an intense and vibrant red.

We filled it with many things we hold dear, in an intentional disarray that reveals a small universe each time one of the many doors of the totem is opened. Every day we give it a different shape, and in the evening, when its mirrored interior reflects the orange light of our seventies lamp, it almost feels like having a lit fireplace at home, in a symbolic and central position as Frank Lloyd Wright might have done.

With ATOMAA and Fabio, the game of designing, which we know well and for once enjoyed experiencing from the client's side, has given us a home that from the first night felt like the most comfortable garment we've ever worn, and one that surprises us every day with a different nuance of its beauty – a beauty that represents us deeply in a way we could never have imagined.

This piece of writing was conceived and orchestrated by ATOMAA and originally appeared on atomaa.eu. We thank ATOMAA, Fabio, Andrea and Francesca for allowing us to share it within these pages.

(Left)

ATOMAA describe the totem as a feature that "speaks and gestures and interacts with its various sides, mirrored towards the entrance, a bar corner towards the sofa and a wine cellar towards the dinner table." Image: Andrea & Francesca.

(Left)

Andrea and Francesca proclaim they have created a place "... where colour is taken seriously. Every element of this house has its own chromatic identity and often expresses it with intense simplicity through a flat colour." the only exceptions being the central reinforced concrete pillar, the tiled floor and the totem. Image: Francesco Stelitano.

Too Good for its Own Good.

When design overachieves.

WORDS KIRSTEN DRYSDALE

<u>I lost a crucial piece of pine dowel recently, while putting together some revolting flat pack furniture. I found a twig in the garden to replace it. It seemed to do the trick – the bamboo shoe cabinet is still standing, a few weeks later, in our entryway. Will it last months? Perhaps even a year or two? Will I loathe myself as much when it inevitably breaks as I did at the time I purchased it?</u>

What do you reckon the people who design flatpack furniture are thinking when they provide you with a handful of soft plastic plugs and flimsy tacks to hold flaky sheets of low-grade MDF together? Are they thinking "this will stand the test of time"? Or perhaps "I wonder how many divorces this will provoke?"

I don't think they're thinking "gee, this is designed so well, it just might put us out of business". That might seem a preposterous hypothetical, in today's throwaway environment, but it is a very real possibility. Every now and then, people really do sit down to make a product as good as it can possibly be – and end up signing their own death warrant. It's happened before!

Go to Scotland, take a few whisky tours, and you'll come face-to-face with a few of these glorious ghosts of enterprise.

Not the whisky itself, obviously. Scotch whisky is the perfect drink, and highly consumable, and will forever be in demand. The distilleries are doing just fine. But many of the malt mills that grind the barley to *make* the whisky are so damn good, so damn sturdy, and so damn reliable, that the companies that made *them* are long gone. Porteus and Boby were the two firms most famous for this Pyrrhic fate. They designed such robust whisky mills that by the 1960s virtually every distillery in operation had one – but then ... uh-oh ... no-one ever needed to buy a replacement. Worse, no-one needed *anything* more from them. The machines were straightforward to run and fairly low-maintenance, and there was rarely even a need for repairs or replacement parts because they were made of such top-notch materials to begin with. So the phones didn't ring, and there was nothing to do, and the mill-making companies had to shut their doors.

Many of these mills still operate in distilleries today, some over a century old – they are solid steel workhorses, rolling and grinding grain into grist, day after day producing the perfect blend of husk, grit and flour for mashing so that we may sip the perfect dram. But today's whisky makers have been left in a pickle: only a handful of people know how to fix the milling machines on the very rare occasions something does go wrong, and if you need another mill, well – where do you go to buy one? Some distilleries have even commissioned brand new mills made from the blueprints of those original machines, requiring only a few minor tweaks to the design to meet modern workplace standards.

Now, I don't own a Porteus whisky mill – but if I did, I suspect it would be my most prized possession. What a special thing – what a treasure!

Experiencing the quiet pleasure of a 'built to last' item is a rare treat these days, but it's one anyone can enjoy with a bit of effort. Hunting down these items becomes a hobby of sorts. It's one I've recently taken up, and I cannot help but evangelise by brandishing my set of laundry pegs at anyone who visits.

They are made of 316 Marine Grade Stainless steel. They cost $25 – about eight times the price of a standard pack of plastic ones.

Absurd? No. They are brilliant. I will never need to buy pegs again. These pegs do not crumble and decay after one summer in the sun. Their hinges do not snap or go rusty. They have been on my clothesline for seven years now, and still look absolutely fresh-out-of-the-packet-brand-new-shiny-and-strong. They are not, actually, expensive pegs – spread over the decades of laundry hanging I have ahead of me, they will work out to be the cheapest pegs I could have possibly found. And they are emotionally rewarding: every time I use these pegs, I feel deliciously smug about how smart I was to buy them.

Now, I don't want – or need – a solid steel shoe cabinet that will last hundreds of years. But for many of my purchases I know there is a happy medium between twig-joined-junk and immortal-mill – and that it just requires a willingness to pay a little bit more at the outset, and to put a little bit of effort into looking after things. It's summoning that willingness and effort that sometimes fails me, but I find inspiration and encouragement in the "Buy It For Life" (BIFL) community on Reddit. This group was created to "showcase high quality, durable and practical products that can be bought once and used for life". Members proudly share advice and examples. There's a guy with a 30-year-old woollen sweater that looks brand new. There are whole discussion threads about which kitchen knives to buy – and how to sharpen and maintain them. There are people who've successfully done their own repairs on 17-year-old coffee machines to avoid buying a new one.

There's something about it all that feels … empowering. Like you're part of a movement sticking it to The Man who just wants to keep you as a perpetual customer. It's no secret that 'planned obsolescence' is widely deployed these days as a business strategy. iPhones that can no longer support the software updates required to run them? A tiny fridge part that fails but is more costly or bothersome to replace than just buying a brand new appliance? Yeah. They do that on purpose. (The 'Phoebus cartel' was one of the earliest, and most notorious, examples of this practice. An international cartel of light bulb manufacturers who got together in the 1920s and deliberately shortened the lifespan of their bulbs, to ensure customers would need to keep buying more of them. Real 'evil genius' territory.)

And so, I now find myself hovering over the "Buy Now" button for a brand of household bins that cost hundreds of dollars each. It does seem crazy at first – but then I think about how many bins I've begrudgingly binned in the last ten years – because the cheap 'steel look' plastic coating is flaking all over the place, or the step-lever hinge has busted - and I think of my perfect pegs, and how nice it would be to have bins to brag about too. The company claims their bins last at least 20 years, which tallies pretty favourably against my long-term bin budget. And they've found a genius way to stay in business: proprietary liners, designed to perfectly fit the rim. Customers can buy the bin – and keep coming back for the bags.

No Glass.
No Pineapples.

No lots-of-things without glass, for that matter.

A pineapple was a luxury in 18th century Europe. The kind of status symbol an aristocrat might display on the centre of their dining table, showing off their ability to acquire exotic delights. The cost of producing just one of these spiky conversation pieces was at one point estimated at £3000. You could even *hire* a pineapple for your soirées for one guinea – a coin containing about a quarter-ounce of gold. Look, the point is this: if you wanted a pineapple outside of South America in the 1700s, it would only come at great expense. But more than money, more than guineas or gold or silver, more than any precious bartering token you may have to offer in exchange for that tropical fruit, there needed to first be *glass* in the equation.

WORDS KIRSTEN DRYSDALE

In the northern latitudes it was cold, and pineapples don't like the cold. There was no price high enough to make a pineapple grow outdoors in Buckinghamshire. (And you weren't going to ship one – it would rot in the months it took to reach you.) But the demand for pineapples drove the development of 'hot-houses', or pineries, to grow them in. The pineapples were planted in stepped beds full of lovely fresh warm horse manure (frequently turned over), while wide panes of glass spanning the walls and angled roofs performed a precious function: trapping the sun's heat inside, keeping this little dung-den cosy enough for the fruit to grow.

Glass is like that. An often overlooked – or literally looked right through – crucial element making the impossible possible. In the Georgian era, sure, it just helped rich people get a taste of pineapples. But in the Medieval period, glass had a somewhat holier mission: it helped poor people get a taste of God.

Stained glass windows were the primary form of pictorial art at that time, and churches were one of the few institutions wealthy enough to commission them. Hundreds of pieces of coloured glass were arranged to depict biblical scenes – illuminated by the light shining through them, they brought mesmerising, kaleidoscopic stories from the Bible to people who couldn't read. Islamic mosques also featured breathtaking stained glass, although their designs used geometric patterns rather than figurative images, which are forbidden by their scriptures.

It is entirely plausible that without glass, two of our major world religions wouldn't have caught on the way they did.

Jump to the current day, and glass is ubiquitous, it's on every building you look at. But even better than bringing us God, it's bringing us God-like technologies that once seemed like magical thinking. Did you just FaceTime your new baby niece on the other side of the world? That was Brought To You By Glass. Had laser eye surgery and can now see? Thanks, Glass. We're adorned in and surrounded by the stuff. It is the key to the connectivity of the modern world – we cannot live a digital life without it. It's our watchfaces and smartphones and TV and computer screens. It's the fibre optic cables that carry information across the internet and deliver it to our watch faces and smartphones and TV and computer screens. You might even be charging all these gadgets with energy from the sun which is converted by the solar panels on your roof. (Glass, you've done it again!) Some even argue that we should label our current era The Glass Age – a time defined by this material.

Anyway – pineapples. The 150 years of "pineapple mania" is now recognised as such a significant phenomenon that it has its own chapter in art history books. (If you want to know just how nuts it all got, look up the "Dunmore Pineapple" in Scotland. This pineapple castle looks like an AI-creation designed to bait boomers on Facebook but is entirely real.) Nowadays, if you want to impress visitors with a pineapple on your dining table, you'd need to drop a grand on a Swarovski crystal[1] pineapple. Which is, of course, *glass*. See? It all comes back to glass. And our connection to glass goes all the way back to the Stone Age...

1.

Glinting in the ground

The first caveman to notice a dark glimmer at the edge of an old volcano would have had no idea he (or she – no reason this couldn't have been a cavelady!) had stumbled upon one of the most important materials for humanity: Obsidian is the naturally occurring form of glass. It is created when lava cools quickly, leaving behind a black[2], brittle, shiny rock. Our Neolithic ancestors worked out that breaking these lumps up in certain ways produced very sharp edges, which they fashioned into arrowheads and blades and scrapers and other tools. Probably not ornamental pineapples, though. One presumes they had higher priorities than that.

Several hundred thousand years later, humans finally went into competition with volcanoes, and started making glass themselves. Glass beads from around 3500 BCE are one of the oldest known human-made glass objects, though they are thought to be an accident: a by-product of metal making found in Bronze Age slag. Whether people in Egypt or the 'Near East' of modern-day Iraq were the first to make glass *on purpose* is unclear. The important thing is *someone* worked out that melting sand mixed with a sprinkling of other ingredients, then cooling it down really quickly, got you glass. Hooray!

1   The term 'crystal' – in reference to decorative glassware – is confusing, because glass is not, in fact, a crystalline substance. Ask a physicist, and they will explain that glass is actually an *amorphous solid*. You will look blankly back at them, and they'll say, "true crystals have a highly organised microscopic structure, glass doesn't". And you'll say "why do we call it crystal, then?". And then a passing historian will explain that it's because in the 1400s, the Venetian glassmaker Angelo Barovier developed a way of making totally clear glass which resembled naturally-occurring quartz rock crystal, so they called it *cristallo*. "Ahhh," you'll say, "So we call it crystal because it looks like crystal, but it's technically *not* crystal?" And then the physicist will say "Yep – and what's even crazier is that glass is technically not a liquid or a solid either. It's kind of its own state of matter." And your brain will hurt and you'll decide that's enough glass trivia for one day.

2   Obsidian is *usually* black. But sometimes it's brown, or green. And very occasionally blue, or red, or yellow, or orange, depending on what impurities it may have mixed with. There are rules, with glass – but many exceptions to the rules.

2.

(1)
Swarovski's crystal pineapple with gold plated leaves.

(2)
To save you looking it up, here's the pineapple castle that "looks like an AI-creation designed to bait boomers on Facebook" and was built by the Earl of Dunmore in 1761. Image: courtesy of the National Trust for Scotland.

(3)
Replicas of hand-knapped obsidian spear points collected in Guadalajara, Mexico. Image: Matt Heaton, courtesy of FossilEra.com.

(Page 202-203)
The biblical scene of The Annunciation depicted in stained glass at Saint Saviour's Cathedral (Sint-Salvatorskathedraal) in Bruges, Belgium. The artist was Samuel Coucke, who completed the work between 1833-1899.
Image: sedmak/iStock.

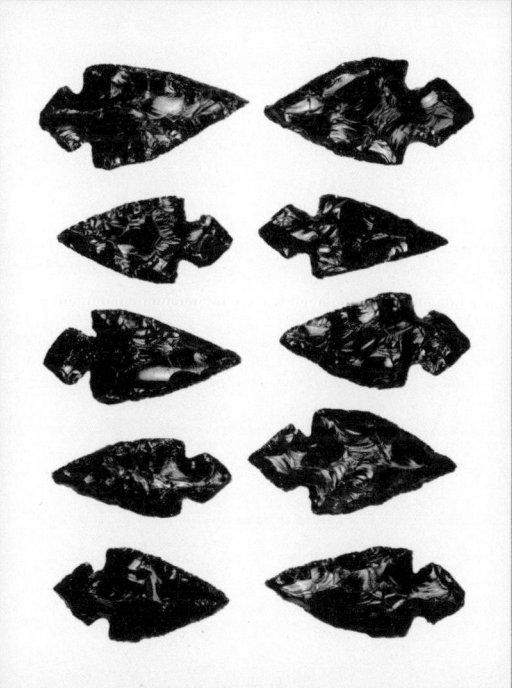

3.

4.

A piece of blown glass is reheated in a contemporary gas furnace.
Image: Daniel Dempster Photography/Alamy Stock Photo.

By 650 BCE, the Assyrian king Ashurbanipal had a 'glassmaking manual' in his library – recorded in a set of cuneiform[3] instructions chiselled onto stone tablets[4]. So, sure, they were literally 'set in stone'. But the truth is any glassmaking 'instructions' should be seen as more of a guide, really, because the whole thing is pretty much alchemy. There are all kinds of chemical mixes you can use to produce glass, and all kinds of different results you can get. The *usual* equation is sand (silica) + soda (sodium carbonate) + lime (calcium oxide) x really high temperature[5] & fast cooling = glass. But you can use quartz pebbles and potash instead. You can adjust the temperature of your furnace depending on the recipe you're using, your glass can be transparent or opaque or coloured. Add a bit of cobalt for blue glass. Or lead antimonate for yellow glass. Or a *different* type of lead to get exceptionally clear glass (or 'crystal', see Footnote #1).

A crazy idea

For a very long time, making shapes out of glass *took* a very long time. You had to pour it (while molten) into a mould, or wrap it around another shape, or roll it across a textured surface to create decorative markings. It produced beautiful objects which were both useful and prestigious – but it was a fairly imprecise and laborious process. So full credit to the Syrian craftsmen who, around the time BCE ticked over to CE, decided to try something new – something a bit crazy: They decided to *blow* on the molten glass, through a long tube. This created a bubble, which could be much more quickly – and precisely – shaped[6] into the desired form. The Romans quickly copied the method and spread it across their Empire, which by all accounts, was rather vast. Glassmaking went from a specialised craft to a widespread trade in an instant.

Different cultures favoured different styles of glass over time, but by the 13th century, no one was making glass quite like the Italians were. The industry was huge in Venice, where local glassmakers were renowned the world over for their skill and quality products, including spectacles lenses.

Unfortunately, the glassmakers were renowned in Venice itself for causing heaps of fires. In 1291, the city's glassmakers and their troublesome furnaces were moved to the nearby island of Murano, partly to distance the fire risk – but also to better protect their trade secrets by isolating them from nosy visitors.

Murano glass was the epitome of luxury throughout the 15th and 16th centuries, exported all over the world, though the secrets of their glassmaking did eventually escape the island and its dominance slowly waned. And now, in the 21st century, used glass from all over the world is coming home to Murano...

Glass waste to paste

One of the best things about glass is it is almost endlessly recyclable. Glass bottles and jars can be repurposed (every nanna knows this). There's a reason you can earn 10 cents in most places for returning a glass bottle: it's rubbish with significant value. Used glass from all kinds of sources –

---

[3] Cuneiform being the wedge-shaped writing system of the time.

[4] These instructions read (approximately): 'Take 60 parts sand, 180 parts ashes of sea plants, 5 parts chalk –– and you will get glass.' This is a fairly small proportion of sand, though, suggesting it wasn't possible to reach high melting temperatures at the time, and that the glass produced was likely soft and suitable for only basic vessels.

[5] Hi – yes – another exception to the rule: some plants produce glass from the silicon they absorb through their roots, but without using heat to catalyse the chemical reaction that turns it into glass. No one knows how this happens. The fine hairs of stinging nettles and the skeletons of ocean sponges are examples of this mystery nature glass.

[6] Don't for one second assume this method was any less stressful. There's a reality TV show called "Blown Away", currently in its fourth season, that is built entirely on the high-stakes drama of glassblowing. Granted, it's a format of contrived *competitive* glassblowing with an additional component of competitive art-wankery – but even without cameras and producers upping the ante, blowing glass involves physical strength, intense concentration, very hot fire (lots of fire) and the ever-present threat of gravity smashing your painstakingly made creation to smithereens.

5.

6.

including building and consumer waste – can be thoroughly cleaned and sorted and crushed and melted back down and turned either into new glass, over and over again, or used as an aggregate in things like asphalt and concrete.

On rare occasions, waste glass is deemed non-recyclable for one reason or another. Even that glass can overcome its fate at Rehub – a Murano-based "upcycling" plant that has developed a way of turning it into a versatile paste, *at room temperature* (a rather more energy-and-emissions-friendly temperature than a furnace). That paste is then pumped through a 3D printer and used to make jewellery, tableware, furniture, lights, tiles, surfaces and decorative objects. It's a brand-new, innovative, patent-pending process. And of course, basing the business on the island of Murano keeps their secrets safe from nosy visitors.

Modern glass

But no one wants to sequester traditional glassmakers away on an island, these days. Their craft is niche-to-dying as far as art forms go – or was, until *Blown Away* re-popularised it (for more on the important patronage of reality television, see Footnote #5). There are special ways glassmaking is being practised, revived and appreciated today – even those Syrians who first filled molten glass with their own breath would find some of it pretty wild.

The Spanish artist, Jaime Hayon, designs astonishing glass figures inspired by decorative African masks. A studio in Murano brings the components for these to life, blowing their main form into moulds and then delicately balancing the colourful adornments of stems and funnels into its openings. Iittala's Finnish glass factory creates musical wind instruments out of glass for the experimental sound artist Damsel Elysium, who said they "could see the sounds when I saw the glass being formed". Architectural glass[7] blocks are making a comeback – but not in the frosted hollow cubes of office buildings or 1980s feature walls. This time, they're cast to create a solid prism the size of a standard brick, then polished until they're ice smooth and crystal clear. The creative and practical implications of fully transparent brick walls (sometimes integrated with regular masonry) are only just beginning to be explored.

[7] The first gift glass brought the world of architecture was windows: before sheet glass was invented, any hole you put into a wall for light and ventilation was going to also let bad weather and bugs and bad guys in. So, those holes tended to be pretty small, and indoor spaces used to be pretty dank and dark. Today, glass's gifts are both practical and aesthetic – and in the hands of an imaginative architect, it will never fail to deliver breathtaking results. The extraordinary Crystal Palace, created for London's Great Exhibition in 1851, was one of the first sizable structures to be made almost entirely of glass. Since then the world has been treated to glass icons including: Berlin's Great Tropical House (1907), Bruno Taut's Glass Pavillion (1914), Philip Johnson's Glass House (1949), Ludwig Mies van der Rohe's Farnsworth House (1951), the Louvre's glass pyramid (1989), London's 'The Gherkin' (2003), and Beijing's 'Bird's Egg' National Grand Theatre (2007). (And yes, it does seem that glass buildings are getting whackier as time goes on.)

(5)
The MINA glass, designed by Murano glassmith Giberto Arrivabene of Giberto Venezia. Image: Andrea Avezzu', courtesy of Giberto.

(6)
Rehub Terrazzo made completely from Murano glass-waste can be easily customised in colour and size. Image: courtesy of rehub.

(7)
Sauda (Dark Beauty) from Jaime Hayon's *Afrikando* collection. The collection is a set of seven glass vessels all inspired by the decorative arts of Africa. Image: courtesy of Hayon Studio.

7.

8.

(8)
Gum Blossoms, cast glass with flame worked glass. Image: courtesy of Lee Howes Glass.

(9)
Glass Matchbox, finalist in the Ranamok Glass Prize. Image: courtesy of Lee Howes Glass.

(10)
Cube Screws, made using 3D print Technology. Image: courtesy of Lee Howes Glass.

9.

In Newcastle, Australia, Lee and Zac Howes – a mother and son duo – use 3D printing to create moulds for glass shapes that would otherwise be impossible to achieve: a glass cube puzzle of interlocking pieces, a clutch of twisted glass cylinders that perfectly fit together. And Lee once created a glass matchbox – complete with a little drawer and matches – through a combination of casting, fusing and screenprinting.

All this cutting edge technology is exciting – but the older glass forms persist, too, and the Howes are helping to keep the tradition of stained glass windows alive. Churches commission the pair to create new stained glass windows, or to repair the ones they already have. Private individuals, too, might ask them to create a bespoke leadlight window, a couple of metres high and wide, to allow sunlight to flood their entryway through the prism of a native flora bush scene. It will take Zac around a month of full-time attention to bring this to life. (He has taken over the leadlighting[8] work, because Lee's blood lead levels are getting too high after 30-odd years of exposure.)

Ask Lee why people are so drawn to glass, and its affinity with light is a big part of her answer:

"It has qualities that nothing else has. The transparency of glass, the luminosity of glass, the glow of glass. No other substance has the same qualities. We just can't get it out of anything else. People have tried to recreate it out of resin and stuff, but it doesn't work – it'll stay for a couple of years, but then it just loses its vibrance."

There are some frosted, coloured glass eggs sitting on the display shelf at the front of her shop. They do indeed glow, as if there is a small light bulb or flame set inside them. People pick them up, look underneath them, try to figure out what the secret is. Zac explains that it's simply the glass catching the light, drawing it in. The glass egg does what the stained glass windows do, then. It transforms light into spectacle.

You won't be surprised to learn that pineapples are a popular motif in leadlight designs. But if I wanted to impress someone with a glass object, I would choose not a pineapple, but one of Lee's handmade glass gum blossoms. She creates each individual stamen by hand, holding a small square of glass over a flame and gently stretching it out to form a long string, which she then rests in a curved mould before firing. Then, each filament is tipped with a small yellow 'glob' of glass, to create the anther of pollen at the end. Hundreds of these are then inserted into tiny holes drilled into the flower's cast glass receptacle, completing the marvel: a delicate gum blossom, made entirely of glass.

The extraordinary detail and fragility of the object forces you to ponder the properties of the material it is made from: its versatility, its mystery, its beauty and many functions – and to note how rarely we stop to appreciate that life as we know it simply would not be possible without glass.

10.

8 Leadlight is an umbrella term that includes stained glass windows. The distinction is generally that leadlight designs tend to use clear glass in geometric patterns, while stained glass is for colourful and detailed pictorial designs. Both styles use lead strips with channels along the edges, to hold the pieces together within the frame. Anyone working with the material needs to have annual tests to monitor exposure.

THE LANGUAGE OF COLOUR

AN INTERVIEW WITH DANIERA TER HAAR + CHRISTOPH BRACH OF RAW COLOR

WORDS KATE KOLBERG

A few minutes into our video call interview, Daniera ter Haar excuses herself to accept a delivery at her front door. The live-work studio home Daniera shares with her partner (in life and work) Christoph Brach is in a formerly abandoned, post-WWII Phillips factory, and with Daniera attending to her package, I am left with an unimpeded view. My eyes move from a red and pink lamp to the moss green plinth supporting it, then the multi-coloured scraps of fabric and paper taped to the wall in rows. And from there I begin to reckon with where to begin a conversation that could account, not only for all these different mediums, but the hues too. Colour, after all, is in their name.

If you're not counting their three full-time employees and one intern, ter Haar and Brach make up the two halves of Raw Color - a Dutch multidisciplinary studio they founded in 2007. The Eindhoven-based studio practices across the fields of graphic design, product design, installations and photography, and in addition to their numerous self-initiated projects, has worked with the likes of Kvadrat, Sancal and IKEA. And the thread that ties all these disciplines and distinct collaborations together? You guessed it. Colour. Along with a singular determination to spread more of its vibrancy into the world of design.

—

Tell us about Raw Color - where and how did it all start?

Christoph: We met at Design Academy Eindhoven, during a "Man and Identity" course to be specific. I had done graphic design beforehand in Germany where I'm from and studied some product design at DAE too. Daniera had a background in visual merchandising. It was after graduating in 2007 that we really began working together in this way.

Daniera: When we started, we made a business card that said Raw Color and nothing else. I guess this is more common today, but it was unusual at the time. We wanted to be a multidisciplinary studio so the benefit of this was that it didn't box us in - it really encouraged a multimedia approach from the start. This mix was what shaped our identity. Colour really became the basis of everything we do, so whether we're working on websites, publications, visual identities, products or exhibitions, we imagine it as the centre point. Colour is our handwriting.

(Page 210)
Loop Collection for Sancal (2022) Image courtesy of Raw Color.

(Left)
Christoph and Daniera in their studio.
Image: Elise Borsboom, courtesy of Raw Color.

(Top left)

IKEA Collection *Tesammans* / rug (2024) Image: IKEA.

(Top right)

IKEA Collection *Tesammans* / trolley (2024) Image courtesy of Raw Color.

(Bottom left)

IKEA Collection *Tesammans* / pot and vase (2024) Image courtesy of Raw Color.

(Bottom)
Link Collection for Sancal
(2022) Image courtesy of
Raw Color.

I love the idea of colour as handwriting. It highlights an important distinction between tool and craft. Like, in the same way that handwriting is a tool to tell stories, you use colour to create visual worlds across different mediums.

Daniera: Exactly. Colour is a language, and it offered us a foundation to work on. It takes way more time than if we were just working in black and white, but it also opens up so many opportunities. You mix new things and you get excited again. It's red and pink – *sure* – but on different materials, so it feels new. There is much more to that though, as well, because it's not as if you can just take the same colour code for a fabric as you could for plastic. There's a lot of trial and error to translating these hues across digital, print, textiles, plastics. And then there's scale …

It's almost as if colour is a language that needs to be translated across mediums and contexts, which must be all the more difficult when working across different cultures and platforms.

Christoph: Colour is, on one hand, a universal language. We all can agree that the sky is blue, plants are green, the sun is yellow. The layer of cultural conditioning can make it complex due to its local interpretation of colour meaning. Sometimes it is impossible to do it right for everybody globally. In our collaboration with IKEA, for example, they shared insights about how yellow evokes positive reactions in countries with cooler climate and less sun, while the same yellow evokes a different feeling in hot countries with a lot of sun. In these situations, we tend to stay close to ourselves. Which combinations do we enjoy and what makes us happy? Hopefully people feel this energy and the good intentions in the designs.

Can you tell us about the Tesammans Collection you created for IKEA? I'm interested in how you made everything work as a stand-alone piece but also as part of a greater whole.

Christoph: Each object is designed to tell a colour story. For example, the lamp is about reflection and absorption of different tones. Dark absorbs, light reflects. The knit blanket is about visual blending of colours in the eye due to small lines. So we do look for nice combinations individually, but across this collection of 20 pieces, we tried to spread the 15 colours used evenly to create that sense of balance.

So where does shape fit into all this? The LOOP and LINK seating you created for Sancal come to mind. It's clear that colour not only plays a role in making these pieces unique, but in directing their form too.

Christoph: Yes, the relation between colour and shape can't be disconnected. If you put paint on paper it has to be in a shape. Shape enhances colour and vice versa, as seen in the LINK poufs. But those weren't strictly about colour, they are also our way of reflecting on alternative furnishing solutions. By breaking down all formal borders, they are meant to be freeing – to trigger anarchic sitting.

Why do you think it's so important to create colourful and playful design offerings?

Daniera: If labels don't produce items, buyers don't buy them. It's sort of a chicken and egg scenario. With more availability, people would dare to do it more. There's another side to it in terms of what you surround yourself with or who you follow online but at the end of the day, it's about being "brave enough". Colour is one of the first things we use to identify something.

"Colour is one of the first things *we* use to identify something. Or, it *will* be the thing that pulls us in: it's the red dress in the *window* that makes *y*ou stop and enter the store, but then once *y*ou're inside *y*ou bu*y* the black one because it's safer."

(Right)
Research as part of Raw Color's *Planum* collection for Kvadrat (2020). Image courtesy of Raw Color.

(Page 218)
Kvadrat | Febrik textile for *Planum* collection (2020) Image courtesy of Raw Color.

Or, it will be the thing that pulls us in: it's the red dress in the window that makes you stop and enter the store, but then once you're inside you buy the black one because it's safer.

Christoph: I agree - people unlearned the use of colour. They seem to be afraid and scared of using it. We have the impression that it can be considered immature and childish. I guess there's a similarity to singing and dancing. Many adults often feel uncomfortable doing this. The thing all have in common is emotional expression, and this could be part of the fear: being different, being seen and being too emotional. We'd like to be part of changing this.

I also wonder whether it has something to do with a fear of making the wrong colour choices or pairings; a fear that things will go out of style. What's your creative process for staying on the right side of colour clashes?

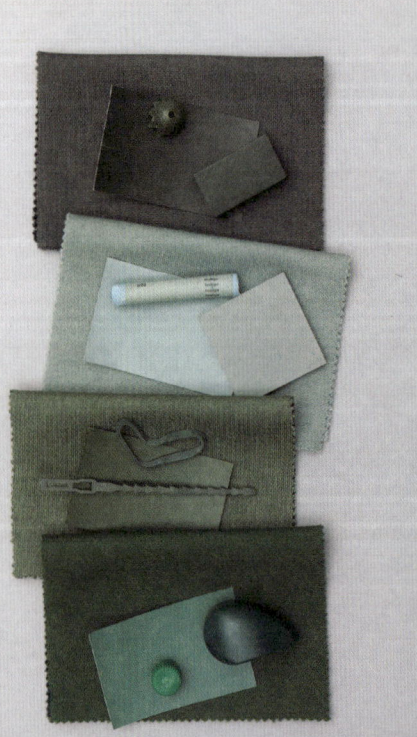

Daniera: In the beginning, we always had a huge research inspiration board for every project, but over time our process has become more streamlined. We have a huge collection of random lids or bottles, brick or wooden bars assembled in what we call our "Colour Library". When working on a new project, we'll refer to these objects in terms of their shape, colour, size, matte or gloss. Then we'll create models using coloured paper to get a sense of how these colours work together at different scales.

Was the Colour Library in use for your textile project with Kvadrat? I read how the inspiration for this palette began with 3D objects. How did you begin to translate those?

Christoph: Indeed. We were inspired by our collection of found objects. Then swatches were painted to understand the construction of colour. These were scanned to define the dyes. Each colour group has four tones to be able to combine - as seen in our LOOP series, actually. Today these textiles can be bought and applied by anybody.

Where else do you turn for inspiration?

Daniera: Anything: daily things, things you see or place together, but beyond that we're always looking at websites, magazines, publications and museums when we can. Our weekends these days are filled with children things (we have two young sons), but if we do go to a museum, we make a deal with them that afterwards we'll go to the sea.

Christoph: We also look to other designers like Ronan and Erwan Bouroullec. It is really brilliant what they have created over the years. The Eames too are fascinating - they have such a wide and beautiful body of work.

Daniera: Oh, and after lunch our team will go out to the park for a 20-25 minute walk. Just being out in nature that's always changing in different seasons is inspiring.

(Top)
Loop Collection for Sancal
(2022) Image: Sancal.

(Below)
Link Collection for Sancal
(2022) Image: Sancal.

The Village in the Sky.

WORDS JAMES SHACKELL

It's probably Europe's most ambitious social housing project: a 14-storey vertical labyrinth that bamboozles all who venture inside. If you think 'apartment living' sucks, well, you never lived in Walden 7.

(Right)
Walden 7's windows are small and uniform as a nod to passive design – on account of the building's inherent thermal mass, there is no central heating. Image: Denis Esakov

Built on the site of an old cement factory in the industrial town of Sant Just Desvern, on the dusty outskirts of Barcelona, Walden 7 is notoriously hard to navigate. Delivery drivers frequently get lost inside it. New residents have trouble finding their own homes. It's not uncommon to see visitors simply standing around, bewildered, like they can't remember where they parked their car.

With its zig zag staircases, suspended bridges, hidden courtyards, and maze-like, honeycomb structure, living in Walden 7 is kind of like living in an MC Escher lithograph. The rules of physics look like they don't apply here. Please remove common sense upon entry.

For architectural photographer Jill Singer, entering Walden 7 was "like walking inside a box where all the pieces seem to move around you. Every corridor seems familiar, yet everything is different, you go up, you go down, you take a few turns and you're as good as lost."

Writing for *Frieze*, Emily Smith was more blunt: "Approached by taxi at the start of my overnight stay, Walden 7 sprang into sight like a vast, jagged red-clay death star."

Built by visionary Spanish architect Ricardo Bofill (and his firm, Taller de Arquitectura) in 1975, Walden 7 consists of 14 floors and 446 apartments – each made up of modular rooms, known as 'cells'[1] – spread over 18 interconnected towers. Each cell measures 28 square metres and can be linked sideways, upways and downways with other cells to form weird, multi-module apartments. The windows are small and uniform. In a nod to passive design and the building's inherent thermal mass, there's no central heating.

> While the exterior is wall-to-wall Catalonian terracotta, the interiors are picked out in bewildering shades of azure, purple, turquoise and yellow. The effect is somewhere between vertical labyrinth and human beehive.

1 'Cells' might sound a bit ominous, but given Bofill's passion for human-centred design, it's pretty clear he's referring to life's biological building blocks here, not, you know, prison.

No linear plane could accurately capture Walden 7's floor plan – for that you'd need some kind of *Star Wars*-esque holographic display. But then, that's kind of what Bofill was going for. Walden 7 was conceived as utopian social housing. A vision of what communal living could, or maybe should, look like. Unlike the grey, brutalist cubes popping up in Soviet Russia, or the functional, prefab apartments of modernist Europe, Bofill imagined something more like a vertical village, slightly detached from reality, where private and public spaces all got jumbled together.

"From the building's interior, it immediately becomes clear that the cells all differ from one another," Taller de Arquitectura's website says. "Not only does each have a separate entrance, but the location of the entrance door ensures visual privacy. In other words, it was not a question of dividing up a large building in the traditional manner, but of creating a series of individual cells that combined to form a block.

"It's as if the architect had taken wooden construction blocks and assembled them on top of and beside one another to obtain an organised yet organic unit."

It's kind of ironic that Bofill became known as a utopian architect, since his structures often feature as backdrops in notoriously dystopian sci-fi movies: his insanely cool and relentlessly colonnaded Espaces d'Abraxas appeared in both *Brazil* and *The Hunger Games*, and Netflix clearly riffed off the pastel pink staircases of La Muralla Roja when designing the sets on *Squid Game*.

Still, there is something inherently cinematic about Bofill's style. His utopianism always came with a twist: it was bold and fantastical, a mix of radical social ideals and dreamlike aesthetics, all wrapped up in a very deliberate sense of *place*. As an architect, Bofill was always more concerned with the Here than the Now. His buildings are direct products of their location, not their time.

"Fundamentally and artistically, architecture is about space and the relationship between time and space," he used to say. "Architecture cannot be translated from one place to another."

(Below)
The "dreamlike aesthetics" of an interior courtyard space within Walden 7. Image: Denis Esakov

Architectural drawings reveal the varied typologies of the apartments within Walden 7. Image: courtesy of Ricardo Bofill Taller de Arquitectura.

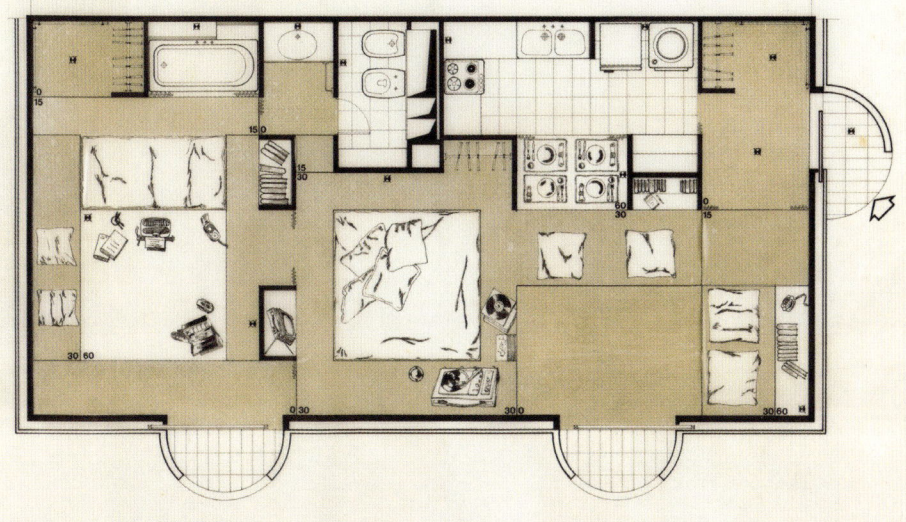

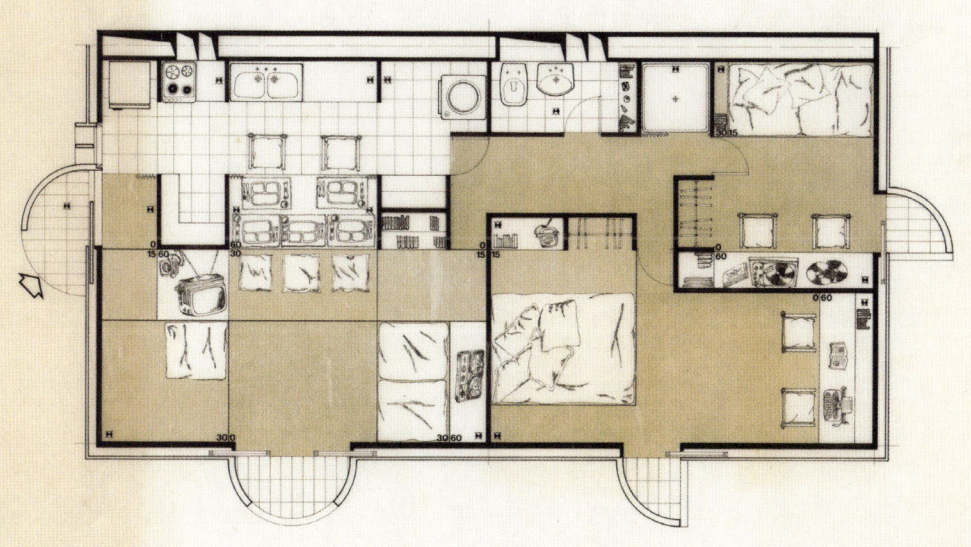

(Below)
Walden 7's communal rooftop swimming pool. Image: Helene Binet, courtesy of Ricardo Bofill Taller de Arquitectura.

(Above and below)
Originally clad in tiles crafted from warm, red-clay terracotta (a nod to Bofill's Catalan roots), after some adhesive issues, a 1995 government-sponsored refurbishment actually replaced most of the terracotta with red paint. This is why, these days, the tiles only remain on the smaller balconies and curved minaret-type structures that run vertically up the building's exterior. Images: Denis Esakov.

(Below)
There are seven interconnected courtyards and four fountains within Walden 7. Image: Denis Esakov.

Ricardo Bofill was born in Barcelona in 1939, just after Franco declared bloody victory over the Republicans. His family was well-to-do and fiercely parochial – Bofill's grandfather, Josep Maria Bofill i Pichot, had been a prominent member of the Institute for Catalan Studies and the Catalan Institute of Natural History. So it's probably no surprise that the young Bofill's designs were possessed of a certain 'sod you' independence of spirit. Technically, he never even completed formal training[2].

> Bofill wholly rejected the rationalism and 'sameness' of mid-century European design. As a born-and-raised Catalonian, with concepts like liberty and defiance against authority drilled into him from an early age, he hated any architecture that treated people like things, or afterthoughts, or anonymous drones in some bigger political game. Humanism was good design, and good design was humanism. A society was only as free as its architecture.

"Walden 7 was, if you like, a critical response to the entire European intelligentsia," he said. "It was a critical response because we said: 'There! It's a monument in the middle of suburbia, a vertical monument in the suburbs!' And straight away there were critics who said: "One cannot experiment with social housing, with architecture for the poor.

"But at the time that's exactly what it was, it was a building populated with people of all varieties."

The construction of Walden 7 took about five years, from 1970 to 1975. The building's complexity extended the timeline, as workers tried to grapple with Bofill's weird, modular apartments, interconnected courtyards, sky bridges and hanging gardens. The original cell design featured a bath in the middle of the room (which most residents quietly removed[3]). In keeping with the futurist-utopia vibe, each of the open-air walkways was named after poets, activists, philosophers and scientists: Jesse Owens, Pablo Neruda, Frank Kafka, Albert Einstein and so on.

2 Franco's Spain was not a cool time or place to be a communist, and in 1957, when he was just 18, Bofill was expelled from the prestigious Barcelona School of Architecture for his role in a Marxist protest. In some ways he never stopped rebelling.

3 I mean, who could blame them.

A 2019 renovation of a two-level apartment within Walden 7 by architects Bonell+Dòriga. Located in the central part of the complex, this apartment's "belonging to the building is practically inescapable, even in its interior. Every one of the apartment's windows frames fragments of Walden 7. Light comes in shaded in turquoise in the northern rooms, more reddish in the south."
Image: Bonell+Dòriga.

(Left)
The terracotta exterior
reflecting its warm glow
into the apartment.
Image: Bonell+Dòriga.

For the exterior, Bofill chose tiles crafted from warm, red-clay terracotta – a nod to his Catalan roots[4]. There was a snag, however. Due to some mix-up with the adhesive, not long after residents moved in, tiles and masonry started randomly falling off Walden 7. This led to long periods of structural repair (and some pretty hairy moments for residents). Bofill didn't seem too fussed about the setbacks.

> "All places of beauty have a very negative side about them," he said. "There can't be beauty where everything works to perfection."

In 1995, a government-sponsored refurbishment actually removed most of the terracotta and replaced it with red paint, which is why, these days, you can only see tiles on the smaller balconies and curved minaret-type structures that run vertically up the building's exterior.

Still, the project was a triumph. In July 1975, Walden 7 made the cover of Architectural Design, and in the years following its completion, the building attracted exactly the kind of people you'd expect an experimental Catalonian social housing project to attract: a mix of young creatives, anti-establishment types, intellectuals, members of the LGBTQ+ community, and families drawn by radical ideals of community living.

Some early residents tried to organise shared childcare, collective dinners and cultural events in the courtyards, and the two rooftop pools were a big hit in summer. Bofill's spirit of experimentation proved infectious, too, with many residents making adaptations and improvisations to their cells, sometimes knocking down internal walls to merge units. As families grew and moved away, cells multiplied and divided accordingly.

This spirit didn't last, however. After 20 years, Walden 7 lost its status as *Vivienda de Protección Oficial* social housing, and a more moneyed crowd gradually moved in. Today, 1000 people call the building home.

"It was supposed to be accessible to everyone, and every resident would have a share," Bofill lamented. "Now it's become a bit more bourgeois – the price has gone up and the community is a bit insular. They don't want to let anybody in."

The name, incidentally, is a reference to a reference. It comes from the novel *Walden Two* (1948) by BF Skinner, which envisioned a utopian society designed to maximise human happiness through social engineering and behavioural conditioning. And *that* book was named after the classic, *Walden*, published by Henry David Thoreau in 1854.

In some ways it's an odd name for a communal housing project, since Thoreau's Walden is – if nothing else – a famous ode to solitude. But Bofill was always intrigued by the gap between the public and the personal, between society and the individual, and the freedoms and responsibilities one owes to the other.

He famously said that, "Architecture is the victorious utopia", which is kind of interesting, since in the original Greek, 'utopia' basically means "no such place". That's the thing about utopias: they don't really exist. The world's not built like that.

But for Bofill, and others like him, that wasn't the point. Utopia was a *vector*, not a fixed position. Architecture really could offer a glimpse into another world, a more perfect world; not just a place to live, but a *manner* in which to live. That perfection may be unreachable, sure, but what a tragedy never even to extend your hand and try.

> "I wanted, once and for all," he said, "to create a space powerful enough to make normal people who know nothing about architecture realise that architecture exists."

---

[4] Terracotta (literally "baked earth") has been used in Catalonia for centuries. Catalan farmhouses (*masia*) and rural buildings often featured terracotta roof tiles, brickwork and ceramics, mostly because there was tonnes of the stuff lying around in areas like La Bisbal d'Empordà.

A DIRECTORY OF COLOUR

Most of us could do with some more colour in our homes and lives. In the event that you need inspiration or solutions, we've curated a list of the brands, retailers, designers and makers who are doing exciting things with colour.

Words Eloïse Lachicorée

1. Our Place
If you're looking for cookware with colour and personality, Our Place's collection of ceramic and titanium cookware and dinnerware is so handsome that you won't want to put it away. Perfect for small spaces short on storage! **fromourplace.com**

2. Montana
The family-owned furniture company Montana has been designing eco-certified, functional and flexible modular furniture since 1982. Its range is available in 41 bold, deep and bright colours to mix and match. **montanafurniture.com**

3. Spincycle Yarns
Initially handspinning and dyeing small batches of yarn, Kate Burge-Tibi and Rachel Price founded Spincycle Yarns in 2004. Their signature "Dyed In The Wool" yarn features slow colour changes and unique blending. **spincycleyarns.com**

4. Amechi
A London-based design brand focusing on traditional African textiles and cultures. Founded by product and furniture designer Amechi Mandi, who is of Nigerian and Cameroonian heritage, he was inspired to launch an interiors brand focused on bringing both playfulness and colour to African design. **amechihome.com**

5. Kvadrat
Regular collaboration with some of the world's most renowned and talented designers has allowed Danish brand Kvadrat to remain a leader in colour, quality and innovation in the design of textiles, rugs and acoustic solutions since 1968. Notable collaborations include Raw Color (see 210) and Patricia Urquiola, with the latter resulting in the world's first recycled polyester upholstery textile made from 100 per cent ocean-bound plastic waste. **kvadrat.dk**

6. Farrow & Ball
Using a precise blend of 12 pigments, and with each new colour undergoing thorough testing, Farrow and Ball has been perfecting its approach to colour and paint for 75 years from Dorset, England. Its range and intensity of colours truly is something to behold and its website alone offers a wealth of inspiration along with services such as virtual colour consultancy and detailed design advice by room and colour. **farrow-ball.com**

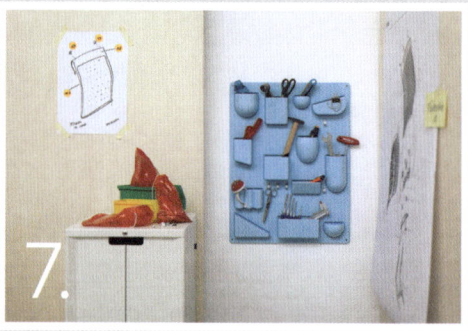

7. Vitra
From Alexander Girard's playful Wooden Doll collection and the iconic Panton Chair to Dorothee Becker's brilliant and versatile Uten. Silo RE wall organiser, Vitra's collaborations with a broad range of renowned designers makes for a unique and timeless selection of furniture and accessories in a delightful range of colours. **vitra.com**

8. Pellington Design
A modular wall-mounted shelf system with colourful bricks, offering both monochrome and custom colour scheme options. The detachable bricks and shelves in the Confetti wall system can be arranged and rearranged to create personalised, colourful shelf creations. **pellingtondesign.com**

9. Dowel Jones
Adam Lynch and Dale Hardiman are the duo behind the colourful and playful furniture from Dowel Jones. Some of their most colourful creations are a result of collaborations with local friends and designers such as the Butterfly Fantasy Foldy Table and the Geelong Weaving Mill Sister Chair. The brand's Thimble stool comes in a choice of 27 colours but Hardiman and Lynch welcome requests for custom colours in this design and others. **doweljones.com**

4. Image: Alexander Edwards, courtesy of Amechi. 7. Image: the Uten.Silo RE II, courtesy of Vitra.

10. HAY

If you've ever walked past the window of a HAY store you will be familiar with the brand's bold approach to colour that somehow manages to land as simultaneously fresh and timeless. Established in 2002, HAY has collaborated with some of the world's most notable designers as a means of bringing great design "to the many" with gems such as Inge Sempé's Matin Table Lamp, Jochen Holz's HAY jug, Naoto Fukasawa's Pao Portable Lamp the the brand's iconic Colourful Crates. **hayshop.com**

11. FUTURE re MADE

Polly Cadden's flat pack pieces made from post-industrial waste require no bolts, screws, glue or instructions. And her range of tables, benches, desks, bedside tables and custom shelving come in a kaleidoscope of colours. **futureremade.com**

12. A.A Danto x India Mahdavi

A collaboration between Alternative Artifacts Danto - part of the historic Japanese ceramic manufacturer Danto - and French-Iranian architect and designer India Mahdavi has resulted in a collection of beautifully pigmented and patterned tiles that showcase natural, traditional and experimental design techniques. **aa-danto.com**

13. Jaime Hayon

Combining bold colours, patterns and organic shapes, Spanish artist and designer Jaime Hayon's work is influenced by both nature and life. From furniture to lighting, ceramics and textiles; Hayon's designs are unique and highly covetable. **hayonstudio.com**

14. CommonRoom

Wallpaper that brings art to the many. Commissioning original designs from contemporary artists, CommonRoom produces an annual archival collection with a range of patterns and designs full of colour and life that celebrate the history of artist wallpaper. Alongside wallpaper, CommonRoom also offers other homewares with a range of artists' patterns and designs. **commonroom.co**

15. In Casa by Paboy

Based in Naples, producing hand-sewn cushion covers in a range of bright colours, sourced from local Neapolitan suppliers, In Casa by Paboy is a social enterprise, founded by Gambian-born craftsman and designer Paboy Bojang. Bojang, who is currently seeking asylum in Italy, employs fellow migrants and hopes to inspire other migrants in Naples. **incasabypaboy.com**

16. Iittala

Finnish brand Iittala has been making exquisite and colourful glassware and tableware since 1881. Some of its most timeless and beautiful designs include glassware designed by Kaj Franck and Aino Aalto and its iconic Aalto vase designed by Alvar and Aino Aalto. The challenge lies in choosing a colour. **iittala.com**

17. Studio Kühü

Studio Kühü is a fashion and textile studio specialising in natural dyeing and bringing colour to textiles and clothing. Using only organic materials and colour-rich botanical materials from the Americas; Studio Kühü offers a sustainable alternative to traditional textile dyeing for both fashion brands and individuals - with a range of natural dyes to choose from. **studiokuhu.com**

18. Image courtesy of Casa Cubista.

18. Casa Cubista

Casa Cubista collaborates closely with traditional artisans, makers and small family-owned businesses in order to share traditional Portuguese design and craftsmanship with the rest of the world. Their collections include brightly patterned ceramics, hand carved wooden objects and linen towels. **casacubista.com**

19. Numbulwar Numburindi Arts

Located in Numbulwar in Australia's Northern Territory, Numburindi Arts is a centre owned and run by the local community. Using locally-harvested pandanus leaf fibre, ghost nets and abandoned fishing line, artists at the centre use traditional weaving techniques to make Wulbung (baskets) and Yir (dillybags) in an array of bright colours and patterns. **numbulwar.com**

20. USM

This Swiss design classic makes frequent appearances in homes featured on Never Too Small. USM's unique and versatile design allows for custom configuration and a range of small-space friendly furniture solutions. The timeless design of the steel ball-and-tube modular frame, paired with panels available in a wide range of colours is a way to add colour to an interior in a way that will never date. **usm.com**

Scan for all the links:

SUBSCRIBE

Sign up for the NTS Sub Club & the shipping's on us!

Yep, that's right: set & forget with **FREE worldwide shipping**.

Scan below or find out more at nevertoosmall.com/magazine